Talk Grey To Me

Written by M'Kai Folley

13TH & JOAN

Talk Grey to Me

Copyright © M'Kai Folley, 2020

Cover image: ©

Published by: 13th & Joan

ISBN-13: 978-1-953156-50-1

Publisher's Note

Printed and bound in the United States of America. All rights reserved. No part of this book may be reproduced or transmitted in any form or by any means, electronic or mechanical, including photocopying, recording, or by any information storage and retrieval system except by a review who may quote brief passages in a review to be printed in a magazine, newspaper, or on the Web without permission in writing from M'Kai Folley.

Although the author and publisher have tried to ensure the accuracy and completeness of the information in this book, we assume no responsibility for errors, inaccuracies, omissions, or any inconsistency herein. The advice and strategies contained may not be suitable for your situation. You should consult with a professional where appropriate. Neither the publisher nor the author shall be liable for damages arising here.

It really does take a village…I would like to dedicate this book to my family and friends who supported me during my greyest hour. When life was grey, you all continued to shine the light.

Contents

Preface 1

Introduction 3

Amara 15

Fantasia 21

Tamieka 29

Sira 35

Jessica 43

Kiara 51

Ro 57

Langston 61

Joel 69

Lucia 73

Stephanie 79

Cameron 85

Alyssa 91

Martez 95

Ashley 99

Isis 103

Nicole	109
Michelle	115
Francis	119
Gabriel	125
Lori-Ann "LA" Stacey	133
Mari	147
Isaac	153
Malcom	159
Camila	165
Hallo	171
Charles	177
Mary	181
Julian	185
Lauren	193
Sierra Leone, American Poet	199
Alison	205
Willie	209
Marie	213
Jada	217
Calvin	221
Leila	225
Tassie	231
Zana	235
Brandon	239

Marcus 243
Emmett..247
End Word..253

Preface

*"Conquering the stumbling blocks comes easier,
When the conqueror is in tune with the infinite,
With every ending comes a new beginning,
Life is an endless unfoldment,
Change your mind, and you change your relation to time."
Play on, children*

—George Clinton,
Band leader of Parliament-Funkadelic
Song: Good Thoughts & Bad Thoughts

Introduction

It's late October and windy outside, with fall leaves scattered everywhere. As I sit in Calabash Teahouse, taking in the warm aroma of lattes and fresh tea, contemplating my life, an email flashes across my screen.

Inbox (1): **FedLoan Services.**

Here I am 24, youthful by any definition, and successful as determined by my master's degrees, yet drowning under mountains of piling debt. It is hard to feel successful at times, mainly because I'm not only in pursuit of my dream career...which right now feels up in the air, but I am also going through an unexpected heartbreak (or *mental shock*, whatever word floats your boat).

While in my period of grey, one of my best friends came to visit me in Washington, DC. Although my friends moved to different cities, we make it a point to visit each other every year after post-graduation. Therefore, when my best friend came to visit I expected nothing but good vibes and laughs.

While the weekend began with laughs and a night of Paint-N-Sip, it ended with me on my knees by my bedside in tears. My friend had just shared with me that a guy I was dating had impregnated a woman and married her.

I've never felt so low, hurt, and confused.

I always thought the first man with whom I've shared my body, would've had the decency and respect to tell me to my face what the current situation was. But, nevertheless, what happened after I heard those words was an awakening.

While my friend was taking a shower, I knelt by my bed and cried. The last time I cried for a man was for Prince…when he died. *Although I never met the man, his music touched my soul.* Anywho, as I heard the shower turn off, I stood up and composed myself. Because I did not want my tears to be taken as a sign of weakness.

I understand now that showing emotion is human nature.

At that moment, I realized I cared a lot more than I led on. In truth, I deeply cared for this individual. However, none of this mattered because what was done was done, and I had to move forward.

During that moment, I kept thinking about the words he would always tell me: "You are in a special place."

What does that even mean? Haha, I should have asked him to finish the end of the sentence. A special place in hell? A special place in the universe? A special place at Barney's? A special place at McDonald's playhouse?

Seriously, where is this special place?

Thinking back to those words now, a special place is a grey statement. There is nothing black and white about it.

Funnily, at the same time I was experiencing a grey area within the professional world. Much time did not pass for me to realize my feelings from both grey areas were coinciding together and making up my current mental state.

M'KAI FOLLEY

Let's just say The Weeknd was on repeat, and I remained at my window.
In the meantime, as I wait for things to fall hopefully into place, I am currently substitute teaching and drinking wine.

If you wanted to take a guess and say my current occupation and mental state may have jump-started my motivation to write this Holy Grail, I would not say you are wrong. I'm just saying if you asked me where I would be six months ago, I definitely would not have said substitute teaching. In fact, I've always told people, *If you ever find me teaching, then something in my life has gone seriously wrong.* Not because I have low respect for teaching—I have very high respect for educators, believe me—it's just not the profession I saw for myself. So as we start this journey, I'm in between internships, substitute teaching, and making just enough to get by. Not knowing when the day will come where my life will fall into place.

So here I am, sitting in Calabash, spending money I don't have but figured buying a cup of tea is better for my body than buying a bottle of wine—and I have an epiphany. (*Not saying I won't buy a bottle tomorrow...*) An aha moment, which is, quite frankly, that we have been lied to... by everyone.

This lie has fostered the "Post-Graduation Utopia" (PGU) mindset.

We attend college for many reasons—to rise out of poverty, gain knowledge, and raise our social status—all in an effort to create a better life we have envisioned for ourselves. Some of us go to college to turn our dreams into reality and some of us go to college to further ourselves. Then upon post-graduation, we realize college may not be the answer to all of our problems.

All our lives, our teachers and our parents have said if you go to college, get good grades, and graduate, you'll get a job, and all's well that ends well.

Newsflash! Not every job a person gets after college is a job they want. Sometimes life interferes, and people are not successful in achieving their dreams.

Those who achieve their dreams know there is no linear line or simple addition for life and success. The formula we have been fed—"college + great grades + graduation= dream job, dream car, and eternal happiness"—is missing variables and mathematical symbols. We got Aunt Sally but forgot, Please Excuse My Dear. PEMDAS, anyone?....proper order of operations is imperative to obtaining the correct value.

Now this formula may be a bit dramatized, but you get the point. If you asked the 18-year-old version of myself where I would be now with two degrees, I would have responded with employers knocking down the door of my New York City penthouse while I sat calmly across the room in my fur coat sipping on the best wine. Instead, here I am six years later, and the only part that seemed to come true was sipping on the wine.

The idea that a piece of paper will exterminate all financial problems and pave the way to utopia is frankly bullshit. But I believed it, and so did my peers.

Upon graduation, instead of entering nirvana, I entered what felt like a dark abyss. While in this dark awakening, I began to seek advice from my inner circle. Hearing what my inner circle had to say, I realized we all have experienced a period in our lives where we felt like we've been in grey areas. Later in this book, I explore their grey areas.

But for now….

WELCOME TO THE GREY AREA.

For the lucky ones who are not aware, the grey area is a period between post graduation and the moment you feel like everything is falling into place. For some people, "falling into place" may look like getting your dream job, entering the military, getting accepted into a graduate program, or even starting a family. However, before you get to your desired destination, there is sometimes a feeling of uncertainty… a state of mind commonly referred to as purgatory—I'm only slightly kidding. For those of you in the grey area (or headed there), the early stages may look like:

- Countless internships or "in-between jobs" to gain experience for the career that you believe four or more years of schooling should have prepared you for. However, after reading through countless job descriptions and a handful of interviews, the world has clarified that it didn't. Even so, when you do land that job to gain experience, you still sometimes have to face and put up with horrible bosses, just so you can get that bomb-ass letter of recommendation and move one step closer in your career.
- Wine, plenty of wine.
- Spending hours or even a summer applying to countless jobs on Monster, Indeed, and USAJOBS only to hear nothing back or have your job application updated to "reviewed" for months, only for it to finally say "rejected."
- Day-drinking and night-drinking… with plenty of wine, of course. Sometimes something harder… and for my

- more herbal readers… something greener and lighter that can take two forms of matter.
- Sitting in your room, in darkness, contemplating your life's purpose.
- Serving as a substitute teacher for a 7th-grade class, which comes with constant reminders to students to not sit in the teacher's chair. And on a bad day, you may have that student to tell you, "I sit where the fuck I want," and you may seriously contemplate jail time… but that's neither here nor there.
- Questioning the loyalty of everyone around you who told you are on the right path and things will soon get better.
- Trying to go through the day with positivity and hopefulness because you prayed to God to guide you, and you know He isn't gonna leave you hanging dry.

It appears the grey area is an adulthood rite of passage, but for some reason, no one talks about it until you're already there.

Feelings associated with this area are, indeed: (1) confusion, (2) anger, (3) hopelessness, and (4) frustration. There are plenty of terms that go along with post-college depression—a social issue that is hardly talked about, although many graduates have experienced it in some shape or form.

> *I mean, come on, losing your student discount at restaurants is challenging. How can the establishment expect me to pay the total price for a burrito with no job, and how dare it consider me a*

regular citizen? Knowing that the next discount you will qualify for is a senior discount is tough on a kid.

When we graduate from college, we are separated from the comforts that college provides. After graduation, we leave behind a community of friends and mentors who readily provide us advice and are expected to be an adult and have all of the answers. Transitioning into the 'real world' without a support system or guidance is rough.

For me, I felt like the dog who went to fetch the ball the owner never threw. I felt lost and confused with a side of frustration. This is because I am a planner. I ALWAYS have a planner in my hand. It's the cranberry juice in my vodka. I knew where I wanted to be but did not know when I would get there. Instead of immediately starting my career as planned, I was interning and substitute teaching part-time and living day by day, not knowing what the next month would look like. This was not me. I'm the person who needs to know day by day, month by month, year by year, and so on with my professional life. Post-graduation, I lived in the unknown, just watching the clock. I wanted to get from point A to B quickly, instead I was going from point A to a.1.

In my frustration, I began writing this introduction, which initially was a rant. I sent the first draft to my aunt, and she immediately called with concern in her voice, asking, "How are you doing? Are you okay? How are you feeling?" These were the questions that someone asks a person they think is on the verge of a mental breakdown. Suffice it to say, this was not the feedback I thought I would receive. Forty minutes later, still on the phone with my aunt, I realized the grey area can be both temporary and permanent.

Yes. You read right.

It is temporary in the sense you will not be in the same grey area twice, fingers crossed.

The grey area is permanent in the sense that we are constantly evolving. Because we are constantly evolving, we need to give ourselves time to process our thoughts and adapt to our current situations and future projections. So, one could say we are always in a grey area because we are always learning.

Remember, growth does not come from comfort zones. Life goes on.

Now, I know it is easy to tell this to a family member or friend. But when you are the one in a grey area, it is so hard to believe. While in the grey, you may feel you are at a standstill and everyone is passing you by..., and due to this feeling it is easy for your motivation to diminish.

Although the grey area may bring unwanted feelings and thoughts, there is some good that comes out of what may seem like the "twilight zone." Amid unemployment, internships, and in-between jobs you think may lead to nowhere and expanding waistlines, you have the gift of time.

See, I'm not all sarcasm and dark clouds—maybe just 99 percent of me is... but just know the 1 percent of me that is the sun... really shines.

Now, I know, I know—Time... really? But, yes. When you are not cramming for a test, stressing over papers, and you are sitting in your room thinking how you got here, you have time to reflect on your learnings and have experiences. Having these reflections help you define your wants, aspirations, and needs more clearly.

College provides you with your degree. That degree is not YOU. Your degree is a tool to help you navigate the world. For instance, you could have a master's in microbiology and have a career as a jiu-jitsu trainer. *This really happened.* A man thought he wanted to cure cancer (which would have been fantastic) but discovered his genuine passion was inflicting pain on others. Now he is a jiu jitsu trainer—and loving it. Therefore, instead of being in the grey area and thinking, *Oh, I cannot wait until this part of my life is over, This is horrible,* or *Why me?* We should use this time to become more aware of our inner selves and discover our passion.

Because, honestly, where are we rushing to?

We are so fixated on time. We always think in terms of "how long." How long will it take to graduate college? How long will it take to complete graduate school? How long will it take to get the job? Then we get the job, and we think about how long until retirement.

Time, time, time.

What did George Clinton say?

Change your mind, change your relation to time.

Let's first understand that time is a concept created by man to give order to a world that does not make much sense. We use time as a tool to abstract black and white from the grey of which life is. In trying to create order from chaos, we have designed clocks and calendars to measure our position concerning other things and each other.

If we can move away from time, then time will cease to exist. The mind is the supreme human tool. Think about how you perceive time in different situations and how the minutes either fly by or drag on forever. Think about the grey area and how it seems like it feels forever. In sum, it's all in our heads.

Instead of thinking about regression, think about progression.

Upon graduation, you are progressing from one stage of life into another.

We have family and friends who have graduated high school, entered the real world, and experienced, or are still experiencing, what we are going through. We, early post-grads, are now getting invited.

So come on in and have a drink. We are all playing the same game.

Do not worry about time. Time is a tool and just that. It is a manmade standard that applies to over 7 billion people in the world. How can we expect 7 billion people to adhere to one standard? We all do not operate on the same clock; we are our own beings and do things on our own time.

> *"Never give up on a dream just because of the time it will take to accomplish it. Time will pass anyway."*

Stray away from social concepts and tune into you.

Trust and believe the seeds you sow, you will reap.

In this grey area, I have learned we take life too seriously. We think about going from Point A to Point B without thinking about the journey between these points. We work hard to work for institutions, companies, agencies who only replace us when we die. Since none of us are getting out of life alive, the least we can do is enjoy the ride and live for ourselves.

For this book, I interviewed individuals with college experiences that include:

- College graduates, both young and old and
- Individuals who attended college and chose not to finish, both young and old.

I hope when you read these stories, you find them relatable and inspiring and able to create conversations within your inner circle. As I stated, we are all playing the same game. In life, it is natural for us to crave absolutes, most certainly because they comfort us. But we are all finding out life is more complex than that, for it is grey.

From birth, our parents, mentors, and teachers have provided us advice on how to live our lives and told us who we are in their definition. Post-graduation, you find yourself on a journey of learning who you are versus who you were made (or told) to be. While on this journey of finding yourself, grey areas will come in different shades and leave like seasons. Just know you will come out on top each time—and if you don't, remember what Cardi B says: "I've been down nine times, but I get up 10."

Understand you are not alone. A piece of paper does not define you. You create your own path. What is meant for you, the universe will send.

Until then,

Play on, Children

Amara

Howard University '16
Penn State, PhD. Graduate Student
Hometown: Los Angeles, California
Age Group: 20s

Life Motto: *"Life is too intricate and nuanced for one life motto. Therefore, 'ain't no life motto' would be mine. What are we, if not a bunch of emboldened hypocrites?"*

LIFE BEFORE COLLEGE

Pre-adolescent, I was raised by my mom until I was twelve before moving in with my dad. Like any other person, I had to contend with personal struggles growing up. However, exposure to both negative and positive environments taught me many life lessons. My parents had a massive influence on the person I am today, and both of their positive and negative attributes played a significant role in my development.

As an adolescent, I didn't know exactly what I wanted to do when I grew up. At that time, I was heavily into arts and loved being creative...but I also had an interest in science. When college came around, I found myself torn between pursuing science or the arts. Although I naturally gravitated towards the arts, I ultimately decided to explore my left brain, so pursuing science became my focal point.

In high school, I sought independence and often felt constrained to my location. As a result, I chose to go to Howard to move away from home to a new state/city and set my path.

COLLEGE OR NAH?

While college wasn't mandatory in my family, I went because what else would I do post-high school graduation? I assumed going to college was the right thing to do. But I think my primary reason for going to college was to get away from home and have a novel experience. I thought of college as a journey. I don't think my decision was based on education itself. I was just trying to embark on a fresh experience and get out of California.

See, at home, everyone graduated high school. Well, not everyone, but many people. Many of my peers went to California State University Northridge (CSUN), which is a state school in the area I grew up in. I viewed that choice for college as a trap. I was like, "Oh, hell no!" I knew attending CSUN would be like attending high school all over again. I knew I would not progress in the ways I wanted to if I stayed close to home. Whereas attending colleges outside of the state, I thought, *Wow, what an exciting new journey.*

When I started college, I attended Howard University and thought, *This is the Black Mecca for real!* Being there was truly amazing. The first thing I noticed was how friendly everyone was. Howard felt like a home away from home. I felt a sense of community that I did not experience in California.

I did not have a four-year plan for college. My goal was to get out of California and explore..and when I arrived at Howard, I did my own thing. Well, at least that's how my freshmen year went. Sophomore year, after my first internship, I realized, *Oh, there is a workforce that I will have to join someday.*

IS COLLEGE WORTH THE DEBT?

As far as paying for college? Loans are the worst! But is it worth it? Loans and all the hard work? Well—that's hard to answer. I have benefitted immensely from attending college, even through just the people I have met. I feel like I would not have had a certain life and academic experience without the people I met along my journey. I think it was meant to be; I would not go back and change anything. However, I would advise others to weigh the pros and cons of college because you are making a major decision about your life, especially if your college of interest comes with a mighty price tag.

My perspective of college has changed from childhood into adulthood. Beforehand, I thought college was what intelligent people do, and now I see how college can be a financial trap. Capitalism associated with higher education is some straight-up nonsense; I think it is messed up because many people have to take out financially crippling loans. Take away capitalism, and I believe college itself is terrific.

THE GREY AREA

I think the grey is an unknowing space and I feel I am constantly in a grey area. But there is beauty in being in the grey area because we are not all-knowing. The grey area is where you experience growth and where you have life lessons. Those experiences and lessons are real—and you cannot necessarily plan them out, for there is no blueprint. For me, I am always in that space where I'm wondering what will happen next and asking myself if I am on the right path? Currently, I am learning to embrace that space of unknowing.

I believe the grey area is permanent and manifests in many aspects of my life. Even when the grey area lies dormant, it seems to always resurface in old or new forms. As I change and grow, the grey area changes with me. The grey area can cause anxiety and stress because it constantly pushes me out of my comfort zone. But again, that's also a thing. My pops always told me to make my emotions work for me, not against me. So when I feel stressed or anxious, I try to divert that negative energy into something productive, even if that productivity means sitting with myself for a few minutes or writing in my journal (AKA Apple Notes).

POST-GRADUATION

After graduation, I was feeling great and very proud of myself! However, I also felt sad because I did not tell my family to come to the ceremony. I did not want to put any pressure on them to go to my graduation, but in the end, I realized I wanted them to be there, especially when I saw everyone else with their family. So graduation was a very emotional but personally insightful event.

Post-graduation, I learned life is more about creating your own path versus school, where everything is structured. You know you have to do X, Y, and Z to get a school degree. However, your primary agenda is primarily set for you by the university. Although I am still in school now, I am interested in finding my own path, and I understand there will be many unforeseen obstacles on my journey.

As for my post-graduation timeline, I did not have one. I knew I would apply to graduate school, so I figured that would dominate my timeline for the next five to six years. Despite being in graduate school now, I am figuring life out as I go. Now, I am in a Ph.D.program that I may or may not finish; I do not know yet.

I view college as a tool to help get you to where you want to go, but it is still up to you to decide the destination. However, college can help you figure out what you enjoy doing and provide the resources to get you on the right track.

While I was not happy having debt, I believe the debt acquired in undergrad was worth having. However, I would not pay for grad school. Not a single penny.

I can, however, say I am satisfied with my degree choice. It is one of those things J. Cole talked about. We aspire and are constantly chasing to have the next thing. We need to have this; we need to have a bigger car. The mindset that 'we need to have whatever'–is leading to our demise. I feel I took the right path, listening to my intuition and staying true to myself. I am proud of myself for staying the course.

Fantasia

HOWARD UNIVERSITY '16, B.A. SOCIOLOGY, B.S ECONOMICS
UNIVERSITY OF MICHIGAN '19,'20, M.S., ENVIRONMENTAL JUSTICE
& MPH, OCCUPATIONAL & ENVIRONMENTAL EPIDEMIOLOGY
HOMETOWN: NEWARK, NEW JERSEY
AGE GROUP: 20s

Life Motto: *"You gotta make time for the things you want in life. Make a plan, but you don't always have to follow it."*

LIFE BEFORE COLLEGE

Growing up in Newark, New Jersey, has given me more reason to get to where I am today. My father was very concerned about my education. For example, if I got a B, he would interrogate me and ask why I got a B, and I had to prove that I tried to earn that B because the course was challenging. If he did not believe me, I was put on punishment. But if I got all As, he would award me $25 for every A, and as I aged, he increased the amount.

    My father encouraged me to realize that education is important. Although I was earning good grades for the money at first, I think my father was strict on education due to him being from where we are from and knowing what could happen if you do not take education seriously. So even though most people would think the area I am from is terrible, growing up in that area was actually a good thing.

My father heavily influenced my perspective of college. As a result, my viewpoint at college did not change as I transitioned from childhood into my adolescent years. However, my view of college has changed from my adolescence to adulthood.

Attending college was never left as an option for me, as it was mandatory for my family. So literally after high school graduation, my options were to leave my parents' house or go to college.

As an adolescent, I aspired to become a doctor, which changed when I got to high school. During my A.P. statistics class, we were visited by a guest speaker who was an actuary and he shared with us his job responsibilities and salary. I became interested in becoming an actuary, so I thought I would become an actuary from my high school junior year until I graduated college, but that did not happen.

COLLEGE OR NAH?

While I was focused on becoming an actuary, I met someone who positively influenced me. My friend convinced a group of us to attend the People's Climate Change Walk with her. So we all went, and I thought it was fun and cool. Although I became interested in climate change and environmentalism, I still wanted to become an actuary, so I did not give too much thought to pursue an education or career in climate change and environmentalism.

Now, attending the HBCU Climate Change Consortium COP 21 talks in Paris, France, turned out to be a jewel for me. I traveled to Paris for COP 21 since I went to the People Climate Change Walk. So it was a good thing I went on that walk!

After my trip to Paris, I landed an internship at DC's DOEE (Department of Energy and Environment). Taking a step and observing my journey, I thought to myself, *Hmm, there are a lot of coincidences.* Then I was nominated to speak at the 4th annual HBCU Climate Change Consortium. While attending the Consortium, I met Dr Taylor, my advisor at the University of Michigan. After giving my talk, she came up to me and asked me about my background, major in school, etc. I explained to her that I'd recently graduated in December and that I was working for Washington, DC's DOEE, to which she responded, "Yeah, that sounds all good, but you should come to Michigan and join the School of Environment and Sustainability and work with me."

I thought, *This lady is crazy; I have a degree in economics and sociology with nothing to do with the environment.* So I ignored her, but she kept telling me to apply, which I did not. Also, the deadline was close and I was not prepared to take the GRE, so I told her I could not apply that year.

Almost two years went by of me ignoring her until I thought, *Hmm. Maybe I should apply.* So I applied to graduate school with the intent of studying economics/public policy, not environment and sustainability.

I applied to all public policy programs except the program she wanted me to apply to. So I contacted her and told her I was going to apply. She told me to let her know when I submitted my application. I applied to all the schools and got into all of them, except for one!

Eventually, I got accepted into the program at the University of Michigan and was initially offered $10,000, but it was not enough money. I said, "Okay, well, thanks for your help, but I cannot afford to attend the University of Michigan." She said, "Do not worry about it; I am going to work something out. I still attended "Admitted Accepted Students' Day", however, I thought nothing of it because I knew I could not afford to attend the University of Michigan.

When I got to Students' Day, I loved it! It was the best visit out of all the schools I visited. But I had to be realistic about debt. So I accepted my offer from George Washington University (GWU) and told my bosses I was staying at GWU and keeping my job, as I was currently working at GWU at the time. Then, three days before the decision was due, Dr. Taylor emailed me to inform me I should receive an email from financial aid and to let her know when I got the email. The next day I received an email from the financial aid office with a fellowship covering my graduate education and was excited.

I attended the University of Michigan because it is a #1 school, #1 program, and I wanted to work with a Black woman. Dr. Taylor proved that she wanted me to come and work with her which made me feel confident about attending the University of Michigan.

THE GREY AREA

Everything that happened between December 2015 and August 2017 was my grey area due to being unemployed. I was too scared not to graduate on time that I graduated early by mistake. I had an internship that lasted until the end of graduation, so I stayed in Washington, DC. When college graduation came, I could keep my internship. However, when summer was over, I still did not have a real job. My boyfriend, Tyrone and my mom sent me money for school because I took classes in the meantime. The grey area was a lot for me.

One day while I was at the dentist, my mentor, Willair, called and said, "Dress up; you have an interview tomorrow." So he got me an interview to be a program coordinator at GWU! So I started working at GWU, and I became more situated in DC. However, once graduate school started, I was back to square one. I did not know where I was going to live, etc. I would ask myself, "Are you really doing the right thing? Leaving a good job and city for a lady you do not know and may not like?" But I got through it.

And yes. I am currently in a grey area, just a different shade of grey.

My experience has taught me the grey area is permanent. The grey area will change between gradients of black and white but will still be grey. If you are not in a grey area, you are either complacent or reached the all and beyond, and I do not think anybody ever reaches the all and beyond, and for me, that causes fear. I have a type-A personality; I need to be in control of my plans. If I do not plan my life, then I have a problem.

HAPPENSTANCE? FATE? OR BOTH

My journey has taught me that some instances are happenstances and some instances are fate. If I did not go along with my friend and attended the Climate Change Walk, I would never have gotten to Paris for COP 21. If I did not go to Paris, I would never have gotten to go to the conference, and if I did not go to the conference, I never would have met my advisor, Dr. Taylor. The events that landed me in my current graduate program at the University of Michigan happened just because one of my friends was nagging me to attend a Climate Change Walk.

#GOALS

When beginning college, initially, I was excited! I do not think I was scared. I was prepared to go off by myself and I was excited to be away from home and away from my parents.

I had a four-year plan that included me graduating in four years with a 4.0, and that did not happen—almost but not there. I was going to become an actuary. First, I was going to study for exams and certifications. Then apply for actuary exams and hopefully, within a year, apply for my actuary job. After that, I planned on applying for a fellowship at an insurance company in Newark, New Jersey, and enter their training program.

Outside of having a lot of work to do, college was fun. It was not as hard as people kept telling me it would be. Mostly, college was what I expected, minus the tribulations of attending an HBCU. Instead, I found college to be a place where you have fun, do work, and have freedom.

As far as paying for college, that was tough. My parents divorced during my freshman year, and it messed up my financial plan a little bit. My mom was smart and put in a clause that required my parents to pay half of my brother's and my tuition if we went to college. Before I went to school, my father asked why I was going to an expensive school. I told him, "You do not need to worry about it; I will figure it out." So, I paid for my first semester of college with my scholarships, and my mother paid for my second semester. The next semester was supposed to be my father's semester to pay. However, I ended up taking out a loan because he was trying to mortgage his house and could not have any loans and needed to have a certain amount of money in his account to get a loan for his mortgage. So I took out a loan in my name, and he said he would pay for it. Then, so on and so forth, my mom and dad split my college payments.

IS COLLEGE WORTH THE DEBT?

The high tuition, loans, etc.? It was questionable while I was taking out the loans, but now that I am paying the loans, I believe it is worth the debt.

Before attending college, I viewed college as a checkbox. I thought everyone needed to attend college to have a job to make a decent living.

Now that I have graduated, I think I was brainwashed about college. I do not think college is for everyone, but I believe it was for me. Academics are generally easy for me. I also understand the amount of debt I ended up with may not have been easy for other people to recover. If you are trying to start a business, you do not necessarily need a college degree, but if you try to go into a specified field, yes, you will need a college degree.

POST-GRADUATION

My post-graduation timeline changed. I did not become an actuary in a year. I am in school again, and I have a completely new post-graduation plan. Nothing happened from my original plan.

Currently, I am a graduate student at the University of Michigan, earning a Master's in Environmental Justice and a Master of Public Health in occupational, environmental epidemiology.

While I have to admit that my undergraduate debt is worth the trouble. I'm not looking to have debt from graduate school.

Disclaimer: I think you need to be very specific and intentional if you enter a graduate program. You should not join a program and not have a post-graduation plan nor understand why you want to pursue post-graduate education. To be honest, I am in this program because it is free. If I were paying for it, I probably would have dropped out by now. It's a great program, and I like it, but grad school is not where you go to find out what you want. You need to find out what you like before going.

And as for me being satisfied with my degree or not, am I content? Well, no, not really because I hate it. I feel like school is something I have to accomplish. Again check the box, so I can do what I really want to do and so people can pay me to do what I want to do.

Here's the deal: college is a system and a bureaucracy built on capitalism that wants your money.

Nevertheless, the lessons I've learned during my post-graduation phase of life were worth it. I realized I should have done whatever I wanted. Take all opportunities that come your way.

Tamieka

B.S. Business concentration Marketing,
Wright State University '09

Hometown: Dayton, OH

Age Group: 30s

Life Motto: "Show the world the true nature of your heart."

LIFE BEFORE COLLEGE?

My upbringing was pretty rough and traumatic. I lived in foster homes and many family homes. I really had little childhood, as I was forced to have adult responsibilities before my time. I started working at age 14. I took care of my three little cousins by helping with homework, doing their hair, laundry, cooking dinner, and seeing them off to school daily. With that being said, I am not a stranger to hard work. But the inner child still wants a childhood. I have strong desires to play, have fun, be free and happy. And this is essentially who I am today. I am a hard-working woman who wants to have fun, enjoy life, and simply be happy. I am no longer interested in working to SURVIVE. I've done that all my life. I'm only interested in careers that I am passionate about that give me energy and allow me the freedom to have fun and create my own happiness.

As an adolescent, I've always had a passion for fashion. I wanted to be a jewelry and fashion designer. However, growing up, I had an aunt who persuaded me to pursue a career that would provide financial stability. Her school of thought was to get the money first and then pursue your dream. As a result, I pursued a paralegal program at my local community college and then later switched my major to business with a concentration in marketing.

THE GREY AREA

Working in corporate America as a double minority was an eye-opening experience. I faced and overcame the glass ceiling most times. Despite workplace inequalities, I was still thriving, but I had to fight for every level of achievement for myself and those I was leading. One day I woke up and decided that I was tired. I was simply tired of fighting inequality. I was depressed and dreaded going to work. So I left the job. I quit an eight-year career with cold turkey and, without notice, just to find another similar one that I walked away from too. I no longer had the drive to do any work I was not passionate about. I no longer wanted to work just to survive. I knew deep in my soul this was not my path. Therefore, I started soul searching and was led back to my childhood dream of fashion and jewelry design. As a result, I just launched my own jewelry business, MiAura Gem Company, which directly aligns with my childhood passions.

It was a hard transition. Especially being a single mother. I did not have the motivation to work a mundane job. So I didn't.

I really didn't know how I was going to survive and care for my son. But my spirit would not allow me to go back to anything that was not serving me during this time. So I took an entire year off and really focused on myself. I went into an interspace journey, and in this time, I found healing and spiritual enlightenment. As for surviving, I did minor jobs that I enjoyed, from acting to Uber, and I prayed. I truly learned how to manifest through the power of prayer and meditation. During this time, I learned my power as a child of God.

One of my favorite quotes is from the late, great Nikola Tesla: "If you want to find the secrets of the Universe, think in terms of vibrations, energy, and frequency." Since energy can neither be created nor destroyed, we have unlimited access to abundance. We just have to tap into the right frequency to access it. I've discovered The Secret, the Law of Attraction. Indeed we can have anything we want in life as long as we do our work from the heart. I desire to share this knowledge with the world through the power of stones. I've recently launched a holistic jewelry business that'll allow me to do exactly that. It's called MiAura Gem Company.

COLLEGE OR NAH?

Unfortunately, to escape my home reality. At 15, I was given a choice to either home school or start community college. My life at home consisted of cleaning, cooking, and caring for children. But it gave me a chance to leave home and experience a different world. I wouldn't say college was mandatory, but I would say it was highly encouraged. Growing up, I used to always equate college to success, which is far from the truth. As a result, I cannot say I've ever used my degree.

I was excited to embark on a new journey when I started to go to college. My family was also excited for me. It was fun, with no real regrets. My ultimate goal was to head to fashion school after my undergrad. I even took a trip to Savannah College of Art and Design in Georgia, visited the campus, and applied for their jewelry design program. Unfortunately, before I could make this dream a reality, my mother got terminally ill, and I married and had a child. Life unfolded before my eyes, and my priorities shifted quickly.

I graduated amid a great recession. There really weren't any jobs for graduates. Baby Boomers were coming out of retirement, taking our jobs, lol. So I did the best I could at the call center. I worked my way up the chain of command and established a strong career in call center management. I ended up staying at the company for eight years. I've made up to $60,000 a year as a call center manager. However, I've racked up $80,000 in college debt. And again, I've never used my degree. The only requirement was the experience. I viewed it as a complete waste of my time. Sallie Mae owes me a refund, lol.

So at this point, I only encourage higher education for technical trades such as healthcare, engineering, or the law. Most industries care more about your experience than education.

IS COLLEGE WORTH THE DEBT?

I used grants and loans, and some scholarships. For me, it wasn't worth the debt. Your credit profile can take you further than education.

POST-GRADUATION?

I was excited about the next phase of my life. My reality differed completely from what I envisioned. It was extremely hard for me to find a job in marketing. I thought I would be successful by having a degree. But I've learned that innovation, good credit, a vision, and execution are what you need to establish wealth and success in America.

I've learned to not put a strict time limit on goals. Man-made time limits will undoubtedly throw you out of alignment with divine timing and cause a great deal of stress. I just desire peace and happiness. I do my base to stay away from timelines because it causes stress and attracts low vibrations. Instead, I now set goals and work toward achieving them without specific timelines or deadlines.

Follow your heart, your passion. Show the world the true nature of your heart. Not the assimilated values that have been instilled in you. When we do work from our hearts, we activate the Law of Attraction and unlock the gates of heaven while on Earth.

Sira

Long Island University, Brooklyn Campus '16, B.A., Journalism

Hometown: Dayton, OH

Age Group: 20s

Life Motto: *"Everything is made up."*

LIFE BEFORE COLLEGE

My family was broke while I was growing up in Dayton, OH. I say it jokingly, but it's true. My dad was one of those people who was really smart but lived in the hood. So, him being really strict, as well as soulful in his teachings, helped me become motivated to not only attend college but to leave Dayton and go to New York. I knew there was nothing left for me in a town like Dayton. Despite the fact my dad wanted us to stay at home, everything he said about life and what was waiting for me after high school was completely counter to my staying in Dayton. I do not think he knew that when he told me though. When I turned 18, I told him why I wanted to leave, and he understood. I love my family, but I did not want to stay in Dayton, OH.

As an adolescent, I was always interested in New York, or big cities just in general. For me, New York glorified this life as an independent professional in the big city. All the TV shows we watched at the time, such as *Gossip Girl* and *Sex in the City* made New York seem so much cooler than any other city to live in. I do not speak different languages, so it made no sense to go internationally for my first year of college. I just knew I had to get out of Dayton. It was to the point where I would not remember the geography of Dayton. My dad was so annoyed when I was learning how to drive. He'd ask, "Oh, you don't know where this is?" I would say, "I am not staying here; I do not need to dedicate time and memory to learn an area I will never be in again."

I dreamed of getting out of Dayton. I knew I wanted to work in media, so I needed to be in either Los Angeles or New York. I picked New York because it was just the influence I was around growing up. New York was also close, yet really far—but closer than Los Angeles to home, so it was a lot more attainable. Plus, my cousin was going to college up there with me, making it easier to decide.

COLLEGE OR NAH?

As a child, I thought all my questions were going to be answered in college and I thought my life would not start until I began college. My life in Dayton was lame, I was lame and I was not athletic…I was pudgy. My family was broke. I was wearing Reeboks from the 29.99 warehouses to school and thought they were the freshest shoes. Since in my mind life would not start until I got to college, I figured I would start from scratch in college.

Okay, so here's my story: when I was in my freshman year of high school, I was disconnected, but I was also great in my classes. When my sister and I transferred to Catholic school, I was still detached, but for reasons related to racism. The white people there were not friendly towards black people. My friends and I ate at an all-black lunch table, and every day we would meet up at the table before classes and for lunch because the school was so white. I even had one person post an embarrassing photo of me, and I will not go into it; just know that it is my Carrie story.

In my time at high school, I thought *I was not going to get good grades.* I was a person who did not care about anything in Dayton, even my grades. But then my dad would see that midterm report and pull me back in! I had to talk to all of my teachers and see how I could pull my grades up. I would average Ds and need to pull them up by B+ or A- by the end of the quarter.

Failing in Catholic school also contributed to the fact that they already pulled me out of my honors classes when I first got there. They pulled my sister and I out of A.P.s because the education curriculum differed from public school. I also think it was because of a race thing. At the end of the day, I just didn't care about my grades.

But, I also remembered my family had no college savings. So, I knew I wouldn't be able to go to New York if I didn't get a scholarship because my family could not afford to send me. So I worked hard the last two years of high school to achieve a 3.4 GPA to get out of Dayton.

COLLEGE LIFE

College was mandatory in my family as well as for many of my friends and classmates. I think everyone I grew up with went to college. I remember being told that if I did not attend college, I would serve my country and start a family on purpose. Unfortunately, I know only a handful who went to college from middle school and another handful who went to jail.

When I got into college, I did not know what I was going to do. But I knew I was going to make a name for myself. Nobody knew me as the lame girl from Dayton, OH. At college I could completely reinvent myself and that's exactly what I did. There were definitely some roadblocks in between. I had eight internships in college, which was fantastic. Looking back to building my resume the way I was building it—I think I was building a good portfolio to get my masters. When I was in high school, I had the same mentality. I joined these clubs last minute in the previous two years because I was trying to get a good portfolio for college.

In college I was hell-bent on lining up internship after internship. Sadly, I was not cherishing my time between internships and building relationships. I thought I would be an assistant editor post-graduation, and now I am a social media curator at a really good company. I also thought I would be out of journalism entirely and work in production at Saturday Night Live (SNL). But I hate production and knew I did not want to work in production. However, I want to work in TV, and now I am in this weird area where I do not know exactly where my next place is.

THE GREY AREA

I would say that since I have been in college, the grey area has definitely been kinda murky. I was in a grey area because I was plugging away and networking. My focus was mainly to get into the media industry. I did not focus on working on getting into the TV industry. I also picked the wrong major freshman year. I did not realize that journalism did not cover all concepts of media. I know now I should have majored in media arts. However, I did not find that out until the following year. So I stuck with my journalism major and tried to find TV internships.

I feel I have been in the grey area for a while. For me, the grey area is basically where you decide on how to take the next step. While I believe everyone is always in this area where their next step is uncertain, I think many people have an idea about their destination.

I found many of the people I aspire to be like have an idea of their next move, for instance, their next movie. I still need more connections in the film and TV industry. I have a job where the people are okay, and the work is acceptable. Although the work has more substance than I had at my previous internship, it is not exactly what I want to be doing for the rest of my life or even the whole of next year.

I do not think the grey area can be permanent. However, it can be permanent because for some people it never ends.

#GOALS

My four-year plan for college was to plug away and work as hard as I could to get a job in the media industry. New York is already such a competitive place. Because, I already went to a no-name college in Brooklyn. I knew I would need to get all the experience I could and all the internships while being a student living in New York City.

POST-GRADUATION

Post-graduation, I was supposed to become a writer or editorial assistant and move from being assistant editor to an editor. During college I set myself up so I could have a couple of options. When I was in college, a part of me wanted to work in the TV industry. So I became a production assistant for *Orange Is the New Black*. I worked my way up the ladder and realized I hated the production and where I needed to be was in the writer's room. I'm still figuring out how to get more connections in the writer's room. In the meantime, instead of following my original plan after college to be an assistant editor, I'm a social media curator in Washington, D.C.

IS COLLEGE WORTH THE DEBT?

For me college is just a vehicle to get me where I want to go. I paid for it with loans. Although it was pricey it was worth the loans. Even though college is a messed-up system that benefits the government more than the youth, I would have never gotten to this point without college. While college is unnecessary for everyone, I believe it is essential for certain people depending on their career aspirations.

I knew already before I went away that college would give me more focus because college is a sheltered environment where you can grow inside before leaving. I knew I was not ready to go out into the real world and work as a production assistant. Simply because I did not know what I was looking for. Also, I needed more of a foundation to go on instead of being in Ohio and graduating high school without a plan. It was not enough to say *I want to work in the TV industry* and go up to New York with no idea how to make it happen.

MY PHILOSOPHY

If I can share any of my lessons from my post-graduation phase of life, I would try my best to stick to the plan because it is easy to get off track. But, if you get the opportunity to be in the field you want to be in and it may not provide you the salary you desire—do it anyway. Pursue passion over money.

Jessica

Howard University '17, B.S. Chemical Engineering
UC Berkeley '18, M.Eng (Nuclear)
Hometown: Mt. Vernon, NY & Atlanta, GA
Age Group: 20s

Life Motto: *"We are defined by the limits we choose to accept."*

LIFE BEFORE COLLEGE

I am originally from Mt. Vernon, NY and my family moved to Georgia when I was a little girl which is where I grew up. I dislike saying I am *from* Georgia because I dislike Georgia. Although my dad is from Roehampton, Jamaica, and my mom is from Montego Bay, Jamaica, they still call Georgia home.

While growing up, my parents were very chill and still are. My parents were not the type of people who would sit around and watch you or would want to meet your parents before you went over to their house. Since they had to work all the time we just ran around and did whatever we wanted. Also, academic and profession wise my parents encouraged us to do whatever we wanted.

TALK GREY TO ME

My dad is a very Christian, Seventh-day Adventist individual. He's very, "Oh, everything you do, you must put God first and pray," and growing up, I thought that was a lot. In New York, I was cool, but when I moved to Georgia, I was *really* bad. I got suspended all the time; I almost threw a chair at my teacher; I walked out of the classroom and walked home because they were getting on my nerves. I even hit the assistant principal. My mom had to come up to the school all the time. Low-key, she was always on my side and saying, "All right, don't be messing with my child." Because ya know, if I tell her the story, it will go in my favor.

I think around high school, something triggered. I did not want to be in Georgia anymore because the environment made me feel stagnant. Since my parents weren't home, I felt constricted. I could not do much because I did not drive, and when you do not drive in Georgia, there is not much you can do. As a result, I felt stuck and planned to graduate early from high school.

My parents encouraged college. They were like, "Oh, that's cool, but also, why do you want to go to college?" Mostly, they did not have input on what I was doing. Not to say that I did not allow them to; they never told me, "You need to do this" or "You should do this." Instead, they were kinda like, "Oh, is that what you are doing? Okay, cool, good luck" or "Let me know if you need help."

As a young girl, I remember I wanted to be a lawyer. Then, at some point, I wanted to be a writer because I was in this speech competition, and that was cool. I wanted to be a doctor, too. I was on a great route to entering one of those professions until I got tired of writing. When I was in high school I took an advanced writing class in British literature and my teacher required us to write many essays. My teacher wanted me to read Shakespeare and other long readings, and I was not in the mood.

Therefore, since I did not want to pursue writing anymore, I tried chemistry. In highschool I had a crazy teacher, but I really liked her, and I really liked her chemistry class. So, I enrolled in a collegiate chemistry class so I could have dual enrollment in highschool and college.

Since, the chemistry class I took at college did not go well for me. I decided to prove I could study chemistry in college. Hence, I majored in chemistry at college, which is how I chose my major.

COLLEGE OR NAH?

College was not mandatory in my family, but my dad suggested it, and he wanted my siblings and me to attend college. I think he would have been happy as long as we did whatever we wanted to do. In the end, I went to college because I wanted to leave Georgia.

When I first got to college, I was like, "Oooooh, we lit! It is lit!" There were beautiful Black people everywhere. *Where are the boys at?* I was not thinking about chemistry. I was just excited to be at Howard University.

THE GREY AREA

The grey area reminds me of being in the middle of nowhere where I am not doing anything productive. I am not behind, failing, or doing something completely horrible. However, I am not fulfilling my dream of doing what I know I'm supposed to be doing.

TALK GREY TO ME

I do not think I am in the grey area but I kind of do. I believe the universe is showing me where I am currently as well as where I'm supposed to be. The universe has already provided me with my next steps.

I believe that the grey area is temporary because eventually, you will find your way into life. The universe will move forward with you and will not be stuck in a period of confusion forever unless you allow yourself to be there. I also think the grey area can be permanent because some people go through life and still feel lost and that's completely okay.

Overall, I think many people experience a grey area. While I have an idea of what I want to do, I do not know how it will manifest. I think the tricky part to me about a lot of this stuff is the level of discouragement that comes with the grey area. I told myself I want to get my PhD or start a business. But I think it is difficult when I know I want to go towards a route and I am being diverted. Not because I am not a hard worker, but because there are people who seek to discourage me. There have been professors saying things like, "I do not think you should do this; maybe you should take another route." Sometimes my growth is stunted by my self-doubt. Am I in the right space? Am I supposed to be here? If I'm not doing great, is this a sign I should cease what I am doing and find something I am great at?

I think the hard part is the constant struggle you will have with yourself. Figure out where I am and what I am doing. Am I on the right path? Should I be here? There are so many other things in life I am passionate about. Why am I putting myself through this? That constant battle with yourself is tough. Before you can overcome anything else, you need to overcome yourself, which can be difficult. When I find myself in such a predicament, I take my friends' advice, go to the park, and sit with my thoughts.

HAPPENSTANCE? FATE? OR BOTH

I do not believe in coincidences much. But, I definitely think things happen for a reason. I believe the universe orchestrates events to happen. Granted, we may not understand the reason at that moment. But I think everything happens for a reason. Life is a journey.

#GOALS

Initially, I planned to graduate and go straight to medical school to become an anesthesiologist. My friend's mother, who is an anesthesiologist, inspired me to become one as well. However, during my junior year, I became interested in pursuing engineering. I had to leave Howard University spring semester of my junior year because school was expensive. So I had to go home that semester and think a lot about what I am doing. *I'm studying chemistry, but do I like it?* During my semester at home, I took a Calculus 3 course and was surrounded by many engineers and thought the field would be cool to get into.

My friend inspired me to pursue nuclear engineering. She got me interested in learning about the environment, and my advisor got me interested in nuclear engineering because he researches nuclear physics at Brookhaven National Laboratory.

I went on a tangent studying nuclear engineering and looking up schools. When I came back to Howard, I thought if I couldn't do nuclear engineering, I could do chemical engineering (since Howard did not offer majors in nuclear engineering), which would prepare me to do nuclear engineering. I remember meeting with the chair department, Dr. Challa, and he said to me, "Oh, you want to study chemical engineering? You should study mechanical. Why do you want to study chemical engineering?" He further said, "I strongly think you should go into the mechanical engineering department." I responded, "No, I already started my chemical degree; I am not starting over." I told him I felt nuclear was more associated with chemical engineering, so that was what I would study.

POST-GRADUATION

After graduation, I was like, "Yo, and I'm out of here! It's a wrap." I was hella hype to be done, especially my last year at Howard. I became tired of certain people. But I didn't realize that feeling can be amplified times a million when I went to Berkeley, and I was like, I'm definitely out of here. I didn't even want to sit through my graduation.

My post-graduation plan is to get a Ph.D. What encouraged me? I met a professor who taught organic chemistry during the semester I went home to Atlanta. He was just beautiful. He went to the University of Florida and has a PhD in chemistry. I told him I was thinking about getting an M.A. He said, "No, you need to get a PhD." I kept saying, "I'll get a master's." He replied, "No, get a PhD. Our people need to be more educated. If we want anything, we can't just shoot for, 'Oh, this will get me there.' We have to go above and beyond because this is how they are going to look at us. You want to be able to run your own show." So that encouraged me to go for a PhD. I am not there yet; I am working on it.

After experiencing college, I think there are bits and pieces that are more valuable than others. I wish I had done more or made better connections with my professors at Howard.

Am I satisfied with my degree? I do not think I am satisfied until I have done what I have set out to do. I am not confident because I am not there yet. I am happy I got my degree; I think it is a real stepping stone.

COLLEGE IS...

College was serious and fun at the same time. While I was at college, I knew I needed to get my degree to reach my goal of becoming a nuclear engineer.

I had a lot of emotions about college. Throughout college, I was working all the time and was frustrated. Although I enjoyed my school courses, I always had a rough time in my lessons. On the other hand, I enjoyed being around Howard's atmosphere. Most of the days, I found myself sitting in the yard and people-watch. Which I found funny because I never cared for people watching... but it felt so good to be there.

I think the way our education system is set up is nonsense. College is another way for the government to make money. Not everyone wants or needs to attend college and that's perfectly okay. Some of the most brilliant people I know are like, "Nah, I'm just not trying to do all that." But then again, some people value their college experience and have found college helpful in their lives. Many of our creations and advancements in our society today were manufactured by people who went to college. Those people all have degrees and made an impact on our lives; due to that, I believe college is a structured way to pass down information.

MY PHILOSOPHY

The lesson that stuck with me the most during my post-college phase is to definitely have a plan, but don't stress so much. Keep an open mind to other opportunities and other things that are going on. Sometimes you can be so focused on everything else and miss what is happening right in front of you. Trust life will work itself out and make sure you are prepared for whatever you choose to pursue in life.

Kiara

HAMPTON UNIVERSITY '16, B.A. POLITICAL SCIENCE
AMERICAN UNIVERSITY, WASHINGTON COLLEGE OF LAW '20, J.D.
HOMETOWN: WASHINGTON, DC
AGE GROUP: 20s

Life Motto: *"Everything will work out on its own. No one makes it out alive. So just don't get caught up in the hype. Your most important thing is to live every day happily. Mental health and happiness are the most important things. I can't express that enough—peace of mind. Never underestimate yourself. Don't focus on what other people have; be happy. Go with the flow."*

LIFE BEFORE COLLEGE

Growing up in DC, the struggles my family faced definitely shaped who I am today. We lived in inner cities and not always in the best areas. However, my mother did not let that type of mindset get into the household. We were always well taken care of and my mom was very focused on academics. I knew early on that school was non-negotiable. She'd say, "You are going to go to school; you are going to go to college." I didn't feel forced because I wanted to attend college, too.

Ever since high school, I knew I wanted to go to law school. I wanted to be a criminal defense attorney, which drove me to attend law school.

At the time, I did not have this incredible understanding of college. Nobody in my family went to school or anything, so I did not understand what all that would imply. I just knew I wanted to go to law school, make some money, and live in a big house. So I did not look at the intricacies.

COLLEGE OR NAH?

I went to college because it was the thing to do. Even though my brother didn't finish, he went to college and my mom went to the University of District of Columbia (UDC) at night. After work, I would sit on campus with her. I viewed college as a means to get money, get out, and do something better with myself. While I knew college was going to be a wonderful experience, I also knew there was no other option. I wanted to go to law school, so I had to go to college to get there. I did not want to join the army or pursue anything else. If I said I did not want to go to college, my mom probably would have pushed for me to go. Not forcefully, because I wanted to go, but she definitely would have encouraged college more than anybody else if I said I didn't want to go. My mother is a unique parent.

As a child, I viewed college as a magical place. So my first reaction to college was like the movies. I'm going to go to college, be in a sorority, have a boyfriend, and we're going to study in the dorm. Then when you get to college, you see… It's a good thing you went and worked hard, but you also see the pretentious part of college.

At the beginning of college, I wanted to do everything. I wanted to make a bunch of friends and do XYZ. I wanted to party and I wanted the *A Different World* experience.

If my child wanted to go to community college and knew what they wanted to do, I wouldn't stress them about going to a four year college and dealing with high tuition.

I look at college as a ticket to get you to the next step. That's just luck. Some people can earn millions without getting a college degree. College is a check on your resume.

THE GREY AREA

My definition of the grey area is the feeling of being stuck if you fail at something. When I started law school, I felt I had imposter syndrome. I would ask myself if I was worthy to be a law student? I had a moment where I thought, *Okay, am I here because I'm the Black girl who got in for the diversity quota?* To prove myself, I tried out for the student court team. It's one of the more prestigious student advocacy teams, and when I did not make it, I found myself in a grey area.

I like to believe the grey area is temporary. So I'm going to call the grey area hopelessness and say that's temporary. Something is going to come and give you hope. If you are alive, you are good, and you have another day to once again feel you are on top.

HAPPENSTANCE? FATE? OR BOTH?

I believe in both. I believe happenstance is the little decision that gets you to your overall fate. I think timing can move in circles. You can make a choice, and ultimately, it's going to get you to a certain place, but everyone's path will be different. For instance, we may all get the same degree in political science, but our paths aren't the same. I think fate is the little nit-picky thing, like remodeling a home—you got a red couch, and I got a blue one. It doesn't make the decision wrong; it's just different.

#GOALS

I planned to go to college, get good grades, get a 4.0 and prepare to go to law school. I applied for law school while in undergrad. I had friends who took a year or two off, but I knew I would get comfortable and probably not go back to school if I took a break. I also thought I would have been married by now and have kids by the age of so and so.

POST-GRADUATION

Post-graduation, I was happy to leave college. I did not see college as a magical kingdom anymore. However, my college experience has made me more grateful. On a personal level, college made me take things seriously. I wish I applied for more scholarships and took advantage of the resources at my college so my mom would not have taken out loans.

Currently, I am expected to graduate in May 2019 and I am not exactly sure what route I want to pursue as a lawyer. When I first went to law school, I planned to pursue criminal defense and then become a judge. Now I don't know what type of law I want to practice. I hope that will change and my passion will become clear to me.

Currently, I'm putting my timeline in a domestic setting. I know I want to have kids before I'm 30, so I'm thinking of doing a judicial courtship or a federal courtship for a year or two, which will help me figure out which law I want to practice.

COLLEGE IS…

A good thing, a world of knowledge. After the first week, I thought the students were the bourgeoisie and sometimes pretentious. In the end, I thought of college as magic and fairy dust and the perfect place.

College gives you a network and fine-tuned skills. But it's a game if you want to play it and it shouldn't be held against anybody who does not want to play. I know people who never went to school but are working IT jobs making six figures.

College is an excellent experience for personal growth. College is great for the person who goes away to be independent, build a network, and make friends; because you can actually make great friends and build a network. When you come from a particular place, everybody in your city or area has the same viewpoint. In college, you meet so many people who have unique attributes you can relate to.

IS COLLEGE WORTH THE DEBT?

I don't think college is worth the debt. College should not cost different amounts of money. The cost of college keeps people from following their passion. If somebody wants to take the time out and attend vocational or trade school, let them do that.

College is an opportunity everyone should have because of the networking and personal skills it provides. Unfortunately, while American colleges aren't for everyone because of the system, the experience is for everyone. American colleges need a revamp; it's a bureaucratic system. I think more schools should be apprenticeship-based.

MY PHILOSOPHY

The lesson I learned after graduation is that networking is so important. You can network anywhere. For example, I was working at daycare while in undergrad, and one of the parents was a defense attorney for the office of a public offender, and he got me my externship. I learned then you have to take advantage of network opportunities. Don't be afraid and don't procrastinate. I'm a procrastinator and trust me... it hinders you in the long run. Don't do it!

Ro

UNIVERSITY OF THE DISTRICT OF COLUMBIA
'18, B.S. MECHANICAL ENGINEERING
HOMETOWN: CHICAGO, ILLINOIS
AGE GROUP: 30s

Life Motto: *"A man is not old until the regrets take the place of his dreams—no regrets."*

LIFE BEFORE COLLEGE

Growing up in Chicago, Illinois, has allowed me to survive, make changes when needed, get resources, endure, and move forward. I think that's the biggest thing growing up in Chicago did for me.

COLLEGE OR NAH?

When I was young, I didn't know anything about college. I just knew I was supposed to go. I thought college was a place you go to make mistakes and believed it was a necessary evil. College wasn't mandatory in my family, so I don't know why I went. I guess because everybody else wanted me to. When beginning college, I was nervous and just wanted to be accepted. I tried to make friends, have a good time...and I did.

THE GREY AREA

As far as the grey area is concerned, it is a mindset that exists outside of time. It can last indefinitely or in minutes; it lies in your ability to recognize you are in the grey area and to leave it. The grey area is an area of indecisiveness and indecision or maybe it's a holding area. The grey area is a place where you figure out where you are and come out with a newfound vision.

HAPPENSTANCE? FATE? OR BOTH?

I believe in both. It's a lot of seemingly random situations that will happen to you and none of it is relevant.

GOALS

I didn't have a four-year plan. I was lost. I viewed college as a place to develop my skills such that upon graduation, I would be ready for what's to come.

POST COLLEGE

I didn't have any post-graduation feelings about my first degree. After undergrad I went to the military because I wasn't ready to go to work yet. There were a lot of lessons I needed to learn before

I went to the 'real world'. I wasn't rushed; I wasn't ready. I was just thinking about postponing having to go to work, so I went to the military.

I felt relieved after receiving my second degree. I was so tired of the process; it pissed me off. There was a bunch of nonsense on every step. What killed me was how I got suckered into so many leadership roles on campus. Subsequently, I had to do all the social activities; I had to learn from that.

Post college I was focused and on the go. I did what I set out to do. My thought process on the situation was pretty much identical; I didn't deviate. When I went to college, I didn't know anything about anything, and I came out knowing a lot of information, and a good percent of it had nothing to do with school or getting a job. So I had to get some more time and learn some more stuff and get myself together.

Now I'm working for Lockheed Martin in a research and design position. So basically, to be honest, I never thought I would have gotten a job here. It's one of those places that's super secured; some of the brightest people work there.

COLLEGE IS...

A necessary evil. I feel like if I had kids that were college-aged right now, I would tell them not to go to school if they didn't want to. I wouldn't force them. I would tell them there are all kinds of things you can do besides going to school, and you will be 100 percent successful if you just do it with passion. I promise you don't have to go to college; it is not for everybody. Maybe you are smart enough to go to school; perhaps it's something else you want to do. I just want to encourage people to do what makes them happy.

MY PHILOSOPHY

Finishing college has taught me that if you stay consistent, you'll accomplish everything. But to be consistent, you have to go through all of your emotions, fail at being consistent, come back to a spot by the grace of God and your passion, and do it all over again.

Langston

HUDSON COUNTY COMMUNITY COLLEGE
'12, ASSOCIATES IN LIBERAL ARTS
SAINT PETERS UNIVERSITY '15, B.A. ENGLISH
HOMETOWN: JERSEY CITY, NJ
AGE GROUP: 30S

Life Motto: *"Life they wonder, can they take me under? Nah, never that"* -Nas

LIFE BEFORE COLLEGE

Off the bat, if I had to talk about my childhood, it would be from a philosophical standpoint. I was born and raised in Jersey City, New Jersey. I also lived in the beautiful Poconos, Pennsylvania. My mom taught me the influences you take on as a kid and to always put certain energy out there. My dad taught me about ancestors and the importance of having Black pride.

See, I always wanted to be an activist. I guess that comes from my parents being the people they are, but I always wanted to be active and spread knowledge and make sure everyone in my immediate circle goes in their circle and learns. I want to learn and I want to extend my want of learning and knowledge to others.

I really love writing, and I grew up in a household where my dad was a professor. My mom was an educator as well. They always pushed me to read but what made me really enjoy writing English were my brothers. My brothers grew up in the hip-hop culture; I always got to hear outstanding linguists. One of my brothers, when he was young, had a crew. They weren't just a usual crew; they actually had talent. Two of them were signed at 14 to major labels. Just growing up in those environments, I had a greater appreciation for what you can do with language and writing. If people don't necessarily like one form, writing has multifaceted outlets.

When I was around 16, my dad was good friends with the great African American writer Walter D. Meyers. Unbeknownst to me, he had me proofread a transcript. Reading that and, first, my dad trusted me to do that, and his friend trusted me; award-winning Coretta Scott King, award-winning writer for young adults made my day; I can honestly do this, I can write.

Picking choices in college, I went with English. Leading up to that point, I was raised for it and directed toward it. However, anything involving writing was my calling; I felt I could share more of the different outlets of myself if I could be a dope writer because I can share my writing with various outlets.

COLLEGE OR NAH?

I went to college because I grew up in a college environment. Attending college was not much of a decision as it was a *This is my next step*. But I also wanted to expand on certain aspects of knowledge and socially what everyone else is thinking. Ironically, I did not go to college straight out of high school; I meandered around. I went to community college for a little bit but didn't really pay any attention during my courses. I was not in a suitable environment. Therefore, I guess the decision to go to college came after I read *The Alchemist*. I realized you have to push things into motion rather than just waiting for something to happen. So I went back into the idea of college being the logical next step for what I wanted to do.

College wasn't necessarily mandatory, but it was the more accepted route. If you were going to college, it was like, okay, you are doing something even if you aren't necessarily working; you are building toward something. But if you had just one job, there was an expectation for me to have a certain type of job. My parents expected more from me.

I always viewed college as a stepping stone. Not one that was necessarily needed for advancement, but definitely helped your advancement in going into certain career fields, especially if you want to go into intellectual forms of workforce and careers.

When I started college, I just wanted to bang out my courses and get out of there. I honestly didn't want to make an extensive profile; I only wanted to get my degrees and leave. So I went to community college and earned my associates, then I went to a university and earned my bachelors. I already felt I was behind, so if I wanted to advance and compete, I just had to bang out and couldn't slack.

THE GREY AREA

I think the grey area is when you realize the narrative you were fed about growing up as a human within American society. When

TALK GREY TO ME

you finally reach that apex or point and you realize it's not real. You realize there is no set definition; you were born American, so this is what you have done; these are the orders, game of life. You are supposed to hit on different pegs. The grey area is a situation where you finally reach a point where you have to write your own story, and it's grey because there is no formula to exit the grey area. Some people take right away to get there, and some take 20-30 years to get there. There's never really a knock on how you get there, just when you finally realize what your calling is.

To reference my favorite book, *The Alchemist*, your legend, when you reach that point of understanding of what yours is, you're not in the grey area anymore cause now you have a directive. I only have the standpoint of being a kid in America. In society, you are force-fed so many narratives of people's lives that are cartoons and movies. Through the representation of the media, you believe you have a narrative. But when you finally realize you don't have a narrative, for instance, when you are 18, you graduate high school, and all these processes that resembled a conveyor belt to push you to this point to get your diploma are no longer there, and now you have to self-push. That's where the grey area is because now you realize you don't really know who you are. There aren't many hands around trying to pull you up and push you to go to class or school or push you to go in to work on time; even if you don't like it, keep going. Those are the grey areas. In the grey area you don't know who you are because, mostly, people have been taking care of you and because of that I think everyone's grey area is relative. The grey area is a point where you have to self-define. I'm in it currently because I still have to self-define.

I believe the grey area is temporary. More so, the grey area is about as temporary as the lifespan. Some people live in the grey area until they expire. It's sad. I look at it like Plato's cave. You want people to be outside of the cave so they can see the cave, but some people never know. It's like a grey area because you really never know where you are at. When people understand they are outside of the cave, some people realize they need to leave the grey area and put in the effort to do so.

#GOALS

My four-year plan was actually five years because I started a year and a semester late, so I had to go over a semester. I honestly thought I would work in journalism or something involving copyrights because it sounds boring for a media company. I wanted to work in an office that would be an excellent standard job to have. I wasn't really thinking about my dream career, which is more of a standard for me than something else.

POST COLLEGE

Post-graduation, I was ready to take on the world. I was prepared to see what opportunities weighed me differently than before I earned my degrees. I felt I was treated differently once I earned my degree. Part of that might be self-conscious; once you get the validation, *Yeah, I can do this,* you walk into the room differently. But, at the same time, I felt people acted in a funny way toward you if you did not have a degree. So it was good to get my education out of the way.

I entered my college path three or four years after graduating high school, so my mindset was different. I wasn't walking in with wide eyes or anything like that. I was walking in, knowing what I was there for, which was to get in and get out. When I first graduated from high school, I was a business major. I took a semester and a half of business classes, and the market crashed because it was 2007. To be a business major within the first couple of years of Obama was the dumbest decision ever. There were many people flipping burgers that were business majors with a bachelor's. So for me to get an associate in this would not be a smart move. When I dropped out of community college, I did not know my next steps. So for the next couple of years, I was a knucklehead with my friends doing hoodrat things. Finally, my dad suggested I look into English or history because I already loved it.

I want to get another degree, but the question is, what? Now I understand, for your masters, it has to be more specialized in the direction of what you actually want to do. Your bachelors can be in whatever. When you go for your masters, it will put your bachelors in focus.

I was reading about Acozi Cortes; she had an economics degree and earned a master's in a field related to law. Her master's degree puts her bachelor's degree in focus. Now she understands the political aspect of finance. Of course, your next degree has to be on the other side of the sandwich to make it all make sense.

COLLEGE IS...

A stepping stone, a couple of pegs on the ladder to get to your next step, even if you don't actively use your degree. There are nonsense classes and there are the classes you actually need. College is your first real experience of the real world and real-world interactions.

MY PHILOSOPHY

Just be honest and understand the power you hold. Maybe because my pops was a professor and a department head, I understood the dynamics of college. But many people walk in thinking college is a place where they are a kid and the professor is an adult. However, when you walk into a college, you are an adult; that debt is going to you, not anyone else. Recognize you are an adult. You give respect to get respect, but there are still two levels of respect—you are giving it or getting it. So don't ever be disrespected, especially for something you are paying for. College is a paying experience; there's a certain level you demand being a paying customer.

Joel

BOWIE STATE UNIVERSITY '11, B.S. PURE MATHEMATICS

HOMETOWN: MONROVIA, LIBERIA

AGE GROUP: 30s

Life Motto: *"Don't forget to smell the roses. We are all out here grinding and doing our things; don't forget to enjoy the moments."*

LIFE BEFORE COLLEGE

I was born in Liberia, West Africa, and came to the States when I was three years old due to the civil war going on back home. I grew up in Hyattsville, MD. My family is from West Africa, Liberia, Ghana, the Ivory Coast, and many of them are still back home, but my immediate family is here.

In African culture, everything is school, school, school, and school again. *Oh, you graduated. Go back to school.* You gotta get five degrees before your parents are even satisfied. But even though my parents pushed education, them being immigrants, they had to work. So my parents instilled a hard work ethic in me. There are no excuses for anything. So I never give up for any reason because we came from something that was a dire situation, and we here now are making it.

COLLEGE OR NAH?

I went to college because, in the African culture, they push school, school, and school. So I knew I was going to go to school. But, my parents would not allow me to just sit in the house. Plus, I thought I was the most outstanding athlete in the world. So I thought I would go to college and become a pro-athlete.

When I was in sixth grade, I had a librarian say to me, "Yeah, right now middle school is fun; when you get to high school, you'll have even more fun, but when you get to college, your experience is gonna be out of this world!" So that right there made me think, *I can't wait until I get to college; this is going to be so much fun.*

THE GREY AREA

When I think about the grey area, a limbo period comes to mind. When you are in limbo, you are going through the motions, trying to figure out if you're on the right path. I would not say you never give up on certain things; you only push it to the background or put it aside for a little bit. The grey area is where you feel as though you have a good idea of what you want to do. Hopefully, you realize sooner than later you are on the right path.

At this current moment, I would say I'm in the grey area. I'm here because I know I don't want to be an appraiser for the rest of my life; I fell into it. I have a good idea, things I know I'm going to accomplish. Have I grown into that person to get to that level yet? I would say no. So yes, I'm currently in a grey area state of mind.

Being in the grey area is very frustrating because you feel as though you are ready for something, and when it does not work out as you hoped or as you planned. It can upset and make you sad and depressed at times, but you still have to press on.

#GOALS

My plan was simple: to get out in four years. When I started, I was undecided. So that first semester, I was unclear on my major. I ended up choosing math and engineering as my major and minor. I still planned on getting out in four years. I failed some classes during that period; it ended up stretching out to 5½ years. The plan was to get in here, have my fun, get my degree, and move on to whatever was next. I did not know what was next, but whatever it was, I just wanted to get out there and earn my degree.

POST COLLEGE

The graduation day was exciting. I wouldn't change anything about my college experience because you meet people you share experiences with.

COLLEGE IS…

A business to make yourself more presentable to companies unless you are going to be an entrepreneur. College is a place where you get your education, meet girls, and hopefully get a good job.

IS COLLEGE WORTH THE DEBT?

Man, if you can get a scholarship, please do that! But was it worth it? Yes, occupation-wise, yes, because I wouldn't be in my current occupation without my degree. As for everything else in life, no, because it is a headache paying back the debt.

MY PHILOSOPHY

From going to college, I learned every day, you learn something new. Do not stress; you are going to be okay. If you are tired and you have an exam in the morning, go to sleep. Be happy; everything works out the way it is supposed to work out.

Lucia

HOCKING COLLEGE OF NURSING '17,
ASSOCIATE DEGREE OF NURSING

THE UNIVERSITY OF CINCINNATI '19, B.S. NURSING

HOMETOWN: COLUMBUS, OH

AGE GROUP: 20s

Life Motto: *"Focusing on me, focusing on myself, and minding my business. You literally can't do anything if you are focused on everyone else's life. So I just focus on my life and what I can do better."*

LIFE BEFORE COLLEGE

So I am originally from Washington, DC, but my parents got a divorce, and we moved to Columbus, OH, when I was younger, so that's where I grew up. Recently I was talking to my sister about how religious our mom was. The church we grew up in was almost cult-ish. We were a part of a Pentecostal church, and it was extreme. I am struggling with how my mom took us from our family and isolated us from Black people. My mind was shaped by living in this church and isolating us from everything; the church controlled our media. I wasn't allowed to listen to secular music. I couldn't watch anything that wasn't Christian-based television; I could only read books they recommended. I feel my upbringing shaped the person I am today. I am a little bit distant from people as I am always somewhat wary of people. I think people always want something versus people just being nice because I never felt such genuine niceness.

As an adolescent, I wanted to be a nurse, and I was gung-ho about it. I originally started out wanting to be a dentist but decided I wanted to be a nurse.

It took me six years to get my associate's in nursing! I went to this small high school in Columbus, OH, where they controlled everything. When I went to college, I was so behind. In math, everyone was like, this is a refresher, but it wasn't a refresher for me. My advisor suggested, "Maybe nursing isn't for you; perhaps you should change the route." So I took on anthropology for a few years. Then I studied to become a physician's assistant until I decided nursing is what I genuinely wanted to do. In my last year at Ohio State, I transferred to a small rural college to get my associate's in nursing. I drove an hour or two every day while working two full-time jobs because I didn't want to give up on my dream.

COLLEGE OR NAH?

I decided to go to college because it is what I had to do. I didn't really have any other option. No one gave me another choice. It was to go to college or go to college. College isn't mandatory in my family now. But when I was growing up, attending college was compulsory.

M'KAI FOLLEY

THE GREY AREA

I'm transitioning out of my grey area. I find the grey area of life is where you do not want to be. If you are in the grey area, you are not where you want to be mentally, physically, or career-wise. But also , the grey area is a place where you have to be because if you aren't in that grey area, you would not know where you want to be.

I got out of an abusive relationship; at the time I was a PCA; I was in school, working, and then suddenly, all of that went away. So it was a horrible time in my life. But then I transitioned, and I was a nurse, and I lost this person I needed to lose. It was scary because I had been with this person for a long time. Therefore, I was in this area where I didn't know where I was going to end up. I didn't know when I was going to go back to school. I didn't know if I would fall back into old habits with that person. Nothing good was happening. It was very grey.

Now I feel like I'm in this place where I've moved on. I'm back in school and I know where I'm going.

When it comes to the grey area, I definitely think it's your mindset. If you decide you want to be in that grey area, then it's permanent. I know people who live in the grey area, and they are perfectly fine. They are perfectly content living in the grey area. But if you decide this is not for you and want more, the grey area is definitely a temporary state.

You know when you are watching *The Wizard of Oz*, the remake, and Dorothy goes to Oz, and everything is in color? That's what it felt like to transition from the grey area. I know I'm not supposed to be here, but I don't know how to get out of here. Then when you do, you know the grey area wasn't all that life was. When you finally get to that color area, you feel great!

#GOALS

My four-year plan was to attend Xavier University, become a nurse, and move to Washington, DC. I wanted to move out of Ohio and back home to Washington, D.C, but none of that happened.

POST COLLEGE

After graduation, I felt I finally made it. Finally, there was validation in me because you think you are stupid when people tell you, you can't do something, but you did. So now I have taken this big test to prove to everyone *not only am I smart enough to pass nursing school, but I'm smart enough to be a licensed nurse.*

Currently, life is moving in the right direction. I'm deciding between becoming a nurse, anesthesiologist or perfusionist. I'm currently working as a full-time nurse, and I'm also going to school for my bachelors and traveling.

COLLEGE IS...

A learning experience. If I had the chance to go back to college, I probably would have waited until I was 18, taken a year off, and gone to community college. Unless your high school sets you up and provides information on colleges such that you know all it can do for you, then take time off until you've researched the university completely. I talked to my sister, and she did not know Ohio State had an allied health program, so I was like, if you don't know all the programs your school has, how can you even go to that school? I felt I needed to go to college, and I didn't know what to do when I got there. So I feel like now, if I could, I would tell my 17-year-old self to do some more research because no one will help you—even when you get to college, no one will help you. Figure it out on your own and do not waste hundreds and thousands of dollars at college being undecided when you can be undecided at a community college and paying a low price.

In my opinion, college is a trap. I think careers should go back to being vocational, where you learn on the job because often, you are not even learning things you need to know in college. Then, when you get out of college and get to your job, they will say everything you learned in college was a lie. Literally, that's how it was for me for nursing. We are here because we have to be here, and everything we are learning is on-the-job experience. *College is definitely for the rich.*

MY PHILOSOPHY

Don't give up! You'll be in this space where you will wonder, *Is this worth it? Should I be doing this?* Once you find your degree, once you find your career, don't give up. Don't let anyone, not teachers, not advisors, not family members, tell you differently. Even if you take forever. If it's something you want to do, it will always be worth it in the end. No money, no amount of time, it will be priceless.

Stephanie

XAVIER UNIVERSITY '10, B.A SPANISH & B.S. NATURAL SCIENCE
XAVIER UNIVERSITY '15, M.S. NURSING
UNIVERSITY OF CINCINNATI COLLEGE OF NURSING,
PHD. CANDIDATE NURSING RESEARCH
HOMETOWN: TULSA, OK & HOUSTON, TX
AGE GROUP: 30s

Life Motto: *"1. Nobody cares about you as much as you care about yourself. So when you are not okay, you need to care about yourself. 2. Roll with the punches"*

LIFE BEFORE COLLEGE

I was born in Tulsa, Oklahoma, but my parents are from Nigeria. I've lived in a few different places. I was raised in an incredibly strict household. We got beat; we didn't go play with friends; that wasn't a thing. School came foremost after God. The only time we played was in organized sports or with other African kids. My upbringing has given me discipline and also has created the focus I have on the school. My upbringing has also helped me to understand the world differently. I know the American set of values is not the only set of true values and not the only set of values that work. But it leads to many cognitive dissonances when you have one foot in one country and one foot in the other. My upbringing has fostered a strong work ethic and a high level of discipline.

In my early adolescence, I wanted to be an ice skater and a woman who plays in the NBA—not the WNBA. I also wanted to be a medical doctor. I thought I could do all three. I didn't understand that wasn't a thing.

I was not athletic enough to be an ice skater. You have to be a ballerina to do that, and I'm not. I also became ill. In my early adolescence, I was diagnosed with an autoimmune disease, so basketball was out of the picture. I couldn't risk getting hit because of the higher risk of organ damage if I got hit or just from playing. Autoimmune disease is a real health condition, so your organs, the heart, don't work the way they are supposed to. Playing a sport is dangerous when you have the type of disparity of disease that I have. That was the main reason I didn't continue with sports in college.

I played a lot of sports when I was growing up. I had to stop when I was advised it could be dangerous. It also meant I was in the hospital almost every week for the last 17 years. I spent a lot of time in the hospital studying, and it just so happens that I'm good with math and science; being exposed to the healthcare field solidified, I was going to pick one of the three goals I had in mind for my career.

COLLEGE OR NAH?

I went to college because I was told to. I didn't choose; you know how most people sit with their parents and have a discussion like,

"You are entering your junior year; tell us something you want to do with your life after high school." Nope. That wasn't a discussion; it wasn't, "Oh, hey, let's think about your life after high school." It was, "You are going to college." Now that I look back, they knew they were sending us to college. But did anybody save money? No, we were scraping by, and my parents felt the only way for their kids' life to be better was to go to school, no matter the cost. However, anyways, it was not my decision. I'm not from a wealthy family; I don't have millions of dollars saved. So I had to go to school, which I mean at the end of the day, I could have said no, but then I would have been out of the house.

As a child, I knew going to college was something I had to do. I knew college was a place where people go, and they learn a lot of stuff fast. As a kid, I always thought college was stress-induced because my mom and her older sister were going to college and all they ever did was be stressed out. So as a kid, I saw that and assumed, okay, I'm going to be stressed out, and that's normal.

When I first started college, I was excited because Manresa (student orientation week) was awesome! I was a little disappointed that I couldn't live on campus because I could tell from the first day at orientation that my college was not a commuter school, so I would miss something in my experience that other people had. So I was disappointed there, but I was so excited. At that point, I made plans to attend medical school. I already had this whole thing set up in my brain about where I was going next. Obviously, that didn't turn out the way it was going to, but it turned out I would get multiple degrees, not just the medical doctor. So I was elated.

THE GREY AREA

I have multiple types of grey areas I operate in. I feel everyone has different definitions. Since I'm a generational American and an immigrant offspring, that's a grey area, an identity grey area. Another type of grey area is the sensation of emptiness while doing things that are supposed to make you feel fulfilled. You think you lack purpose because you are not where you think you should be. So I am in that grey area right now.

I think the grey area comes and goes. I don't think you can ever completely get out of it because we are all searching for our purpose in life, and you never really find out what it is until maybe you die. I'm not even sure if people like Bill Gates or Elon Musk know what their purpose in life is.

For me, I don't think the grey area is temporary. It's permanent with fluctuation. It's a process; it's not like school. You get your stuff, and you are done, but you never stop learning. The grey area is our drive to do better and get better at whatever we aim to do. So the grey area is permanent, but it has variations.

#GOALS

My four-year plan turned into five years. I planned to get my Bachelor of Science and natural sciences and get a major in Spanish to graduate in four years. Then in my third year, I took the MCAT and failed it and threw it in the trash because I broke it with my intellect; that didn't happen. I was going to make lots of friends. I just planned to dominate. I didn't have any other focus other than *I'm going to destroy every class*. That's literally what I had in my head for myself. *I'm going to demolish the school.*

POST COLLEGE

After graduation, I was like, what the F just happened?! If I could have embodied an emo style, I would have. I had a lot of angst. That's literally how I felt. At that point, the entire plan was in the trash. I graduated a year after I had my transplant, which was not planned. I was so sick the year before I graduated; it was terrible.

I went to school thinking *My autoimmune disease is trying to go away; I'm going to be great; I'm so excited.* However, my autoimmune disease took me and threw me in, just washed me, rang me out, and tried to ruin me. I was sick throughout college. I thought I was going to be fine.

Instead of going to medical school, I ended up working at a cancer center in my new hometown. It was awful to work there. I hated that job. My boss made me feel like I was an animal of some sort. So then, after I left, I worked at a hospital, not using my degree at all. So I went from a job where I was using my degree to a position where I wasn't using my degree at all.

Now I'm a registered nurse. I have three degrees. I'm working on number four, getting my Ph.D. I teach, I tutor—I do a lot of things.

COLLEGE IS…

A place where you go, and you learn about yourself and what you can take and what you cannot take. I thought college was where you gather these friends and hang out over time; I think it was a good growth opportunity. I believe that if I had known about the debt, I would have either dropped out of school and worked to get the money or alternatively found a cheaper school to go to. I think college is worth the debt because now I am headed in the right direction.

MY PHILOSOPHY

The biggest piece of advice I'd like to share is to press on, be not weary, for your rest will come. Also, do not get discouraged when you are unsure where life is taking you. Try your best to not get stressed out.

Cameron

Indiana Institute of Technology '16,
B.S. Computer Engineering

Hometown: Dayton, OH

Age Group: 20s

Life Motto: *"Be true to yourself. I like to be honest, straightforward, don't like to beat around the bush and be secretive."*

LIFE BEFORE COLLEGE

My mom was a significant influence on me growing up. I grew up in a single-parent household. So everything I am today is what I saw her do. A lot of independence, doing things on your terms. She was very certain about what she always wanted to do, no matter what anybody else told her; that influenced me to get out there and do it.

I did not have a dream when I was growing up. I think it was the influence of being from Dayton, OH. I saw things and the people around, in school; they didn't know anything, and they didn't want to do anything; this influenced me to want more.

I was really depressed during those years. Again, it is the mentality of Dayton itself, especially at that age, the people outside of the students I met at a program called Upward Bound. Upward Bound helped me a lot more than anything my school ever did. People in my high school weren't sure of anything they wanted to do; looking back now, none of them did anything outside of Dayton.

Post-high school graduation, I still did not know what I wanted to do; I went along with what people were doing. People were going to college, so I did it. I thought, *Well, I got good grades. So I guess college is what comes next.*

COLLEGE OR NAH?

I went to college because my mom told me I did not have a choice. I didn't know what else to do; I knew I didn't want to stay at home and go to work. Going to college would have to pertain to a big fear of mine, and that's living from paycheck to paycheck. I have seen it; I don't like it, and I fear it.

I had a lot of mixed feelings and thoughts about college—a combination of things. Everyone told me college was the next part of my life. However, partying was on my mind. Play around; you got all the freedom in the world; this is freedom. The first time you lived on your own, technically speaking, so I was like, "Yo, let's clown!" Unfortunately, I don't think my mindset was ever to hit the books back then in those first couple of years. It was more so to get through college and not fail.

THE GREY AREA

My definition of the grey area is trying to match things you *like* to do and things you *will* do. You are trying to match up things you are good at doing and the things you enjoy doing. Now those things don't always match up! Sometimes it sucks; even though you like it, you kind of suck at it.

Is the grey area temporary or permanent? It depends on how flexible your mindset is. How much effort you are willing to put in to know what you want to do and match it up with how good you are at it. Never have a mind where you can only think one way. As long as you have the willpower to do it, there is always a way for something to be done, in my opinion. Maybe that's my way of always being a hopeful person. There's always a way for something to get done.

HAPPENSTANCE? FATE? OR BOTH?

Bit of both. More karma than fate. For karma, it goes back to that positive and negative feeling/energy that you give out. The more positive you and your surroundings are, the more good things happen and vice-versa with negativity. The influence of that feeling/energy determines/shapes how everything works out. Happenstance because you can't expect karma to affect everything in life. The world was chaotic at the time. Nothing can control that.

#GOALS

My four-year plan was to go to classes. The first couple of years were rough. My goal was to work during the summers and winter;

focus on a class during the semester because I was easily sidetracked. If I worked during classes, I would get very caught up in working. I was one of those people where I just worked, and if I started work, I would stop attending class and just work because I was making money now.

POST COLLEGE

I officially completed my classes in December; my graduation was not until May. However, I had a job and did not want to go to graduation. I felt I did not have to prove anything to anybody with a piece of paper. But you know, I felt the need to influence the next generation. I had a family with young cousins who wanted to see me graduate, which I understood, and it was the only reason I attended the graduation.

Honestly, if I didn't get a job after completing my classes, I would have been disappointed. This interview would have been a whole other conversation. But everything worked out, and I'm in my next part of life. I'm working as a researcher at the University of Dayton Research Institute. I work for the government as a contractor as well.

COLLEGE IS...

A mixture of culture and fun; the college will always be fun unless you make it un-fun. At the same time, college is a trap. A lot of classes seem unnecessary in the long run of things and the money. It costs too damn much. You see these loans, Jesus Christ! So it's a bit of a trap, in my opinion. Outside of that, the college experience is priceless, and college is a place to build relationships. A lot of friendships you start from college last longer than the ones from high school. College is a miniature world of its own with everything.

WAS COLLEGE WORTH THE DEBT?

Ask me after the debt is over. I would say it's a debate; it depends on how long you were in college. For me, honestly, because I know, I will make enough money, yes. One of my friends from college went and became an elementary school teacher; she is not getting paid anything. So she stopped being a teacher and got paid more by being a banker.

MY PHILOSOPHY

Stay on track as much as you can and have fun. As soon as college is over, life gets real.

Alyssa

HOWARD UNIVERSITY '16, B.S. BIOLOGY
UNIVERSITY OF MICHIGAN '22, PHD. ECOLOGY
& EVOLUTIONARY BIOLOGY
HOMETOWN: WEST ORANGE, NEW JERSEY
AGE GROUP: 20S

Life Motto: *"It could always be worse. Everything will be okay; I won't be poor and end up on the streets; I just need to be grateful for what I have."*

LIFE BEFORE COLLEGE

I grew up in the suburbs of West Orange, New Jersey, which gave me an educational advantage. My parents were very strict with me, which helped me develop into a very rigid, disciplined person. A lot of my family was involved in my educational pursuit and anything else extracurricular I did.

When I was a teenager, I wanted to become an artist. But I did not know what a career was. I liked the art class, and I knew I like to do sketches and express myself. However, my mother had a different version of success. She told me I should become a doctor, mainly because of financial security. I fell into that because she's my mother, and I thought mothers knew best. So she helped me apply to a school that we thought had the best program to get me into medical school.

I became a biology major at Howard University. She helped me shadow different doctors she knew. I grew to hate the idea of being a doctor because she shoved it down my throat, but I needed to assist her with paying for undergraduate expenses, so I started the research program. My research program was in the ecology and evolution program department, and it was amusing, so I took that alternative.

COLLEGE OR NAH?

To be honest, I just went to college because everyone else was going, and I thought I should probably go. My mom told me I should, and she was helping me; I felt I was floating.

During my childhood, I didn't know what college was. I had no clue that college was a thing until I became a teenager, and my parents defined it. I always imagined myself in college, so it didn't change how I thought of it when they told me college existed.

THE GREY AREA

The grey area is a feeling. You feel as though you aren't attached to something, or you don't belong. Or you are unsure if your path is going to lead you in the right direction. The grey area is when you have a lack of connection to something else.

The grey area is very temporary. It comes and goes within seconds, within your thoughts, with times and events. So you can think, *I really love that career option,* or *Oh my God, I should really break up with that guy,* and then you change your mind within a few days.

Failure is the biggest struggle, no matter what kind of a grey area it is. Whether it is a familial relationship, a romantic one, or a career one.

HAPPENSTANCE? FATE? OR BOTH?

Fate. I enjoy believing that forces are pushing and pulling me through life. It makes me happier to believe in fate, so I'd rather be pleased than think things are randomly moving through time. It would bore me and make me wonder if death would be blank and unmotivated.

#GOALS

There was no four-year plan; I just wanted to graduate. So I followed the plan the school gave.

POST COLLEGE

After graduation, I thought, *Wow, what am I going to do?* I was lost. Two weeks after I graduated, something came, and I felt relaxed.

I had two different ideas of what my life would be like. One was restricted, and then when I got to graduation—it was very unrestricted. So I thought, *live your life; you will get paid and be fine.*

Now, I am a PhD student studying Evolution and Ecology at the University of Michigan, Ann Arbor.

COLLEGE IS...

A place where everyone is pressured to go, and you'll have the best time of your life, but also it's the place you should figure out what you are going to do after college; that should be your end goal.

I viewed college as another version of high school, with a lot of freedom. College is a good place for people who want to learn how to network. However, I don't think college is necessarily a good reservoir for much knowledge. In college, it is easy for you to become marginalized if you don't know precisely what you want to do.

MY PHILOSOPHY

If there's a lesson I would share, it would be that you don't have to have everything together. You also don't have to think that what you are doing right now is what you'll be doing for the rest of your life.

Martez

Wright State University '16, B.A. Organizational Leadership, & B.A. Business Commerce

Saint Mary's University of Minnesota '20, M.A. Human Resource Management

Hometown: Akron, OH

Age Groups: 20s

Life Motto: *"Mark 9:23. Everything can be done from he who believes."*

LIFE BEFORE COLLEGE

Growing up in Akron, OH, I had access to experience the visual performing arts. When I was younger, I wanted to be an entertainer. High school sports were okay, but I was happier playing my saxophone. Having a lot more friends in music and bands influenced me to pursue music.

When I got to college, I walked into baseball at Wright State, but I stepped into DJing and continue to work in the music realm to this day.

COLLEGE OR NAH?

I think the only reason I went to college was due to the educational stature of my high school. Once senior class came, teachers were more like, "Where are you going to school at, what college are you going to, what major?" So all of my friends were going to colleges in either New Orleans, California, or Akron; none of my friends went to trade school, community colleges, or certification programs. So college wasn't mandatory, but it was pushed upon me.

During my childhood, I thought college was the end all, be all; a degree is what you had to do to get the things you wanted. Now looking back, I noticed it's a lot more biased. You can get the same thing in certifications or trade school. Whom you know and how you know them can get you a lot further than your degree.

THE GREY AREA

I usually use the words "grey area" in a relationship sense; my definition is attributed to relationships. So not knowing the time, place, and space you are at with these other individuals or where you guys are heading, or how the relationship is going.

I would define the grey area as the area of the unknown—an area where you are uncertain about life. Life takes you to a certain path; the universe, the relationship, or however you want to view it, it takes you to a certain path. You get led on your journey, but you just have to go based on faith. Something I always went by.

#GOALS

My four-year plan at college was to join the baseball team, then work my way up to the starting position. I wasn't thinking about anything else other than baseball. I never gave myself a post-graduate timeline. I've always lived in the moment.

POST COLLEGE

I was glad to be done with school. I never walked across the stage as a graduating senior because, in my mind, I didn't need a graduation ceremony. I was done with my classes and trying to figure out what was next. Even with internships and co-ops, I didn't feel college helped me understand where I wanted to be next. Those things never accurately indicated my full strengths or a sense of my workable and individual strengths.

Post-graduation, I got accepted into my master's program. Currently, I'm an HR assistant for a brokerage company. However, I just interviewed with the IRS, so I'm trying to break through to the government because they pay a lot more.

COLLEGE IS...

Beforehand, college was more of a move to continue my sports background. I didn't think of anything other than sports. Now, I feel college is mostly exploration and finding out who you are as a person. What excites you and what interests you. College is a time for self-exploration of your passions.

Certain aspects of college were great, and certain aspects were a waste of time. If the general education portion of college were shorter, people would find college a lot more interesting.

MY PHILOSOPHY

Never stop. Always continue to do something. Always continue to see growth. Whether it be within your circle of friends, community events, joining youth leadership boards, or youth leadership collaborations. Young Black professionals continue to grow, making connections within your job. Make sure you are constantly growing—further education into your life with your spirituality.

Ashley

XAVIER UNIVERSITY '15, B.A. SPANISH, B.S. PSYCHOLOGY
THE UNIVERSITY OF MEDICINE AND HEALTH SCIENCES, 1ST YEAR
HOMETOWN: CHICAGO, IL
AGE GROUP: 20s

Life Motto: *"Psalms 23. It's just saying that you are going to go through the trenches, but God got you. So don't worry about people who misused you and the negative things you said about yourself. In the end, it's all gonna be good."*

LIFE BEFORE COLLEGE

Growing up in Illinois and St. Louis was a little interesting. I had a good childhood. However, my family is rigorous and enforced discipline because of the various racial issues we experienced throughout my childhood. I encountered people putting dead animals in my mailbox, a boy calling me nigger, and many other things. Those events forced me to learn how to communicate and not harbor ill will toward a specific group of people. In addition, my parents taught me I have to be 10 percent better than my counterparts, causing me to believe I had to be perfect in every way, which is an impossible task in hindsight.

I wanted to attend Harvard undergraduate and medical school. Someone told me attending Harvard was not possible, and because of my past educational endeavors, I believed it, causing me not to apply. The only reason I attended Xavier University was, ultimately, because they were giving me the most money. Then somebody told me I shouldn't even look at a medical school, and that was the moment I stopped accepting no as an answer.

People will always tell you what you can and cannot do and what you can and cannot accomplish in life. So when someone tells you what you can and cannot do just because you think differently, bring your A-game.

COLLEGE OR NAH?

I went to college because my father gave me two options: military or college. The marines on top of that, and he told me this when I was in elementary or middle school. So college, for me, was a must.

When I was younger, I went to this school called IMSA, a math and science academy. I looked at it as an opportunity to get out of a negative educational situation I was in. Mentally, I wasn't healthy when I was younger, and science drew me into learning something new and different.

I thought college was like Hillman College (*A Different World*) and BET's College Hill. I thought college was a place where you could find yourself and do whatever you wanted to do.

I was excited when I first started college. Finally, I was one step closer to going to medical school. I was like, *Ahh, I'm almost there.* But really, I found out, *Ahh, I am not!*

THE GREY AREA

My definition of the grey area is when you know what you want to do, but you don't know how to get there. You try your hardest and go through different avenues to get from Point A to Point B, and the grey area can take you from Point A to C to D to E and then back to E. Life is not always a straight line

The grey area is not permanent. However, you'll never have the same grey area twice. There are different kinds of grey throughout life. Sometimes things are going to be great. But there will also be times in your life where you will not know what you are doing or where you are going. I think that's what makes life… life.

#GOALS

I planned to transfer to another medical school in the US and get into an ER residency program.

POST COLLEGE

I was excited. I was happy my parents could see me graduate because I was the last one of my siblings to cross the stage. I was nervous, though, because I didn't know what was going to happen after graduation. Post-graduation, I knew 'life' was about to happen. I was scared because I knew I was not prepared. My grades and MCAT scores were not where I wanted them to be, and at the time, the best option was to move back home, which marked the beginning of my grey area. At the same time, however, I was excited to know I accomplished a big goal of mine despite being at ground zero.

After college, my original plan was to go into my residency and get matched to a hospital, but everything changed. Marriage goals changed. Friends changed. Everything changed.

Now I'm in medical school. I go to the University of Medicine and Health Sciences in St. Kitts. It's my first year. I'm praising God and pray that I pass every class!

COLLEGE IS...

College is real. It is a place to learn who you are as a person. Do not forget, you are there for a reason. Soak up everything they offer, even things they don't let you know about. You don't need to go to a $40,000 a year school to get the same education. Attend a university that will not only offer you a good scholarship but has the resources to help you accomplish your career and personal goals. If you enter college and do not know what you want, that is fine. College is a black hole; however, be receptive to all college offers, and you will discover your spark.

MY PHILOSOPHY

Don't allow your current situation to affect you mentally. When you allow situations to affect you mentally, you miss life; you miss the things around you, and you miss yourself.

Isis

HOWARD UNIVERSITY '17, B.S. APPLIED MATHEMATICS

UNIVERSITY OF CALIFORNIA SAN DIEGO '19, M.S. IN COMPUTATIONAL SCIENCE, MATHEMATICS & ENGINEERING

HOMETOWN: DALLAS, TEXAS

AGE GROUP: 20s

Life Motto: *"Commit to discipline, and consistency will follow. That's something I made up through different things that I heard."*

LIFE BEFORE COLLEGE

I was born in Queens, NY and raised in Dallas, Texas. I feel like I had a good life. My family wasn't necessarily financially stable, but you wouldn't be able to tell by the life that they gave me. I went to an African private school, so I learned about Black history and Black culture. So my mindset about Black excellence has always been just that—Black excellence. I was in dance classes; I was in gymnastics; I was in karate; I was in the theater. Somehow, my parents could work it out to where I could do extracurricular activities. The different experiences I've had all shaped my current mindset.

I feel my dream as a kid was to stay in the arts. I wanted to work in after-school programs or in some form of teaching outside of the classroom and also do something with mathematics. So I want to teach, but not teaching inside the classroom, only outside the classroom.

COLLEGE OR NAH?

Honestly, I decided to go to college because my mother always said that I would. Originally, from high school, that was the saying: *You are going to go to college.* Then once I was in high school and applying, college became a way out. I wanted to be free and live my own life. Because if I didn't go, the choice was to stay home, which wasn't an option for me.

I thought college was parties, and fun, fun, fun, which it was. But then I learned college is what's going to help me get a career.

The first day of college was exactly what I was expecting. The freedom! I got to live my own life; excitement! Mainly because I went to an HBCU. Being around all Black people just felt really, really great. Going to Howard University feels like you are at a family reunion, and everybody is just coming together for greatness.

THE GREY AREA

The grey area is when someone is not necessarily following their passion and is following what they think they should do, which leads to confusion.

I wouldn't necessarily say I'm in the grey area right now. I could be in a couple of months because I'm finishing up with school. So

I have an idea about what could happen, but I'm leaving space for change.

Personally, for me, the grey area would be temporary. I adapt to different situations. So if things are going one way, I'm not tied down to this having to happen in this exact way.

HAPPENSTANCE? FATE? OR BOTH?

I believe in the mix of them both. Fate, as in certain checkpoints of your life are supposed to happen or will happen, and the in-between is happenstance. You have the choice to decide how you will get there, and if you are listening to yourself, you will guide yourself there.

#GOALS

I wasn't thinking about a four-year plan when I first started college. Coming along the first week of school, I planned to go in, do what I have to do, and then get out. So I can't honestly say I was planning life decisions for post-graduation.

When I began college, I didn't have a timeline. When I was a year in, I had a couple of options: I was going to get my MBA and become a business analyst or business consultant because I wanted to go into business.

POST COLLEGE

Post-graduation, I needed to figure out if I would apply for jobs or go to grad school. I received some offers to teach but was not sure if it was something I wanted to do. I also applied for one school and ended up getting into the school I applied to. I was trying to decide what I wanted my career to look like. And I still wasn't sure. I didn't know where I was going or what I was going to do. I didn't know what state I was going to be living in at all. I was just going with the flow of things. You know, looking at all my options and taking the best one.

My post-graduate thoughts are to use my education to get what I want in life, which means not only a career. That means also networking and using my career to do what I want. Not allowing my career to be all I get with my degree.

My original plan was to get my MBA and become a business analyst. But as far as careers, that's not what I want to do; I plan to do something in tech, like robotics. Honestly, I keep telling my mom I'm going to retire when I'm 35, and that's precisely what I'm going to do. So I want to get into the technology industry, then work hard for about 10-12 years, all the while starting my businesses.

I am currently getting my master's degree at the University of California San Diego in computational science, mathematics, and engineering. I'm working on building my hard skills so I can be marketable. I'm focused on a career right now and my math YouTube channel.

COLLEGE IS....

A place for people to experiment. If that means trying to decide what career path and taking classes in different types of areas to do that or saying I don't like who I am, I'm going to work on myself to experiment with myself physically and mentally challenge myself to test my limits. It's a bonus to get a degree. A college is where you test and challenge yourself to be the best in anything you can.

At times, college is a party. But mostly, I think college should be a place to network, and I can't necessarily say this about graduate school, but depending on your major, it's so simple if you just do it right. And don't procrastinate! College is not as hard as we make it seem.

MY PHILOSOPHY

If I had to share any lesson about college, I guess it would be about managing your time correctly and optimizing your time. I'm a big fan of motivational speakers, so a lot of times, I hear college is the best time of your life, especially if you don't know what you want to do. Do anything, and everything that you might think you want to do, especially if you have no commitment, no family, no children, and are not tied down to any location. If you're going to travel the world, do that. If you want to start a business, do that. If you're going to be in a band, do just that. Whatever it is you think you want to do, go out and try it. In addition, do it to the best of your ability.

Nicole

Bachelors in Social Work, University of Cincinnati '15
Master of Social Work, Boston College '17
Hometown: Cincinnati, OH
Age Groups: 20s

Life Motto: *"Do your best. Don't be upset if things don't happen right when you want them to happen. Be okay not being exactly where you want to be. Nobody's life ever turns out that way unless you are super lucky. But everybody has to go through a bit of struggle to get their dream."*

LIFE BEFORE COLLEGE

Growing up in Dayton, OH, with a single mom made me want to do the opposite of what everybody else did. Because my mom didn't go to college and had a baby right after high school, she struggled with being a single mother. My grandmother started having children when she was in high school. I listened to them talk about having all these dreams and blaming everybody else for their problems and not pursuing their dreams. I knew I didn't want to work all the time, with hardships back to back. I want a life where I can go on vacation. I never had a family vacation. I wanted to do these things I always dreamed about, so I was like, "I have to do something different."

I didn't really have a dream. I knew I wanted to go to college because I wanted to get out. However, I didn't have a specific career in mind that I wanted to do. I just wanted to make money. My mom always told me nurses make good money, so I tried to copy her and go down her path. She wanted to be a nurse and never could be a nurse. So I was like, "Maybe I should be a nurse."

In my junior year of high school, everyone was talking about college. I had an aunt who started taking me on college tours. She started saying how important college was when I was a junior in high school, which was ingrained in my head.

COLLEGE OR NAH?

I decided to go to college because I wanted to finally have enough money to do what I wanted to do. My mom never talked about college as a child, so it was never one thing I thought about. When I was in high school, I started talking about college; I knew people went to college, but I thought, *What is college?* I went from not knowing much about college as a child, then becoming interested in learning more about college throughout high school.

When I first started college, I thought I couldn't do it. I did not feel competent enough. So I began college taking remedial classes before taking the regular courses. Not all of them, but I had to take remedial math. I ended up studying and testing out of the math course because I didn't want to be in the class. I didn't want everyone to think I didn't know what I was doing.

THE GREY AREA

The grey area for me is unmet expectations. I wanted to be an adult who loved their job. "I'm gonna love my job; I'm gonna go to work every day. It's gonna be great." I still haven't found a job I like. I'm still working a job I don't want to work because I need money and moved, and when I moved, I had to start all over again. I feel like I'm going to be in the grey area for like five years.

I hope the grey area is temporary. I'm pregnant, so I have to keep putting things on pause. Employers aren't friendly to people who have newborn babies. So now I'm thinking, *Do I want to work full time and do the job I want to do or do I want to work part-time and be there for my child?* However, I still want to work because I have dreams.

So that's what I'm battling now; I'm hoping it all works out. I'm at the point right now that whatever happens will happen, and everything will be great.

HAPPENSTANCE? FATE? OR BOTH?

I believe in fate. I'm hoping and praying that these things that I'm doing now will get me to my ultimate dream and tell my story one day. I want to say that I started here, and I didn't give up. I'm trying not to give up, but it's hard.

#GOALS

The only plan I had when I started college was to finish. After graduation, I thought I was going to have a car right away. I don't know why I thought I was going to have a job the next day. I thought I was going to be living in a lovely apartment. I thought I was going to take a trip to a foreign country. I don't know why I thought I was about to be rich, maybe because I had two well-paid degrees.

After graduation, I was delighted! I was happy to be done with it for the first time. The first time I graduated, I knew I was going to grad school; I got accepted and everything right away. I knew I was going to a different college; I knew I would stay on the same stage for a while. I was finally doing the whole traveling thing I wanted to do. I moved to an unfamiliar state; I always wanted to live in Boston. I was living my dream. Then I had to face reality.

Things aren't always going to work the way I want them to. So I just have to live in the moment and not always think about what I want to do in the next couple of years. I'm still pursuing dreams, but I'm not constantly thinking about my goals all the time.

Right now, I'm a therapist. I am working with dying people, which is nice, but it's not really what I want to do. The good news is I've always been able and blessed to have a job. I've always had a job in my career, but I haven't gotten paid as much as I want to get paid.

COLLEGE IS....

A door that might open opportunities, but there is no guarantee that college will open a door of opportunity for you. College gives you a chance if you don't have a chance. Even though things aren't working out the way I would like, I would do it repeatedly. I would think more about my degree first. I would get a degree that would pay well and do more research because I feel I was trying to pursue a dream and not thinking. But I think if you don't have the resources and don't have the structure, you can open up doors for yourself if you go to college. You meet friends, get to know people, and even though my plans aren't the way I want them to be, I feel I am in a better place than I would be if I hadn't gone to college.

MY PHILOSOPHY

Focus on making connections as soon as possible. Your contacts will help you get to where you want to be and have a plan afterwards. Have everything figured out? Be honest with yourself. Talk to people who will be honest with you. Do your best. College is a chance, but you'll have to be okay with things not happening right away.

Michelle

MIAMI JACOBS JR COLLEGE OF BUSINESS '86, MEDICAL ASSISTANT

HOMETOWN: BROOKEVILLE, OH

AGE GROUP: 50s

Life Motto: *"I really don't have a life motto."*

LIFE BEFORE COLLEGE

I was raised in the country on farmland in Brookville, OH. I was around the farm, not necessarily on a farm. But I worked on a farm, growing up dehusking corn. I kind of don't freak out about things outside that other women would generally freak out about. I was raised with two brothers, so we were outside all the time, and I am okay with nature. My upbringing shaped where I am today because I don't think I could ever live in town. I'm used to doing things on my own. My mother was an influential person with strong values; she could do anything and everything, which wasn't always correct, but I got that attitude myself; there is not much I won't try.

As a young girl, I didn't dream about the direction I wanted my life to go. I guess I started in my junior year of high school wanting to be a medical assistant. So before that, I never really thought about my dream. I never imagined having kids. Never imagined that, which is odd. However, my rebellion led me down a different path.

I went to a trade school to get out of home and get married because that's what I thought I needed to do. I felt I needed to be married right away. I thought I'd get a job in my field right away, but I didn't. So I started working at the hospital and only stayed there for a short time until I found another position. I stayed there for 21 years.

During that time frame, I got divorced and met my current husband; I got married and had kids. I realized I needed to be home for the kids, so I switched jobs. I worked from home for a while and changed careers to another company. So basically, just one thing after another, life then kids, now my kids are in college. I'm going through empty nest syndrome. Life is coming back to hit me.

COLLEGE OR NAH?

In my junior year of high school, I went to Mayo Clinic in Rochester, Minnesota, to get checked for a skin disease I have on my arm. I saw someone walking around and doing things; I asked about their job role. I followed that person around at the clinic and realized that's what I wanted to do. I wanted to be involved in medicine. Before that, I did not know.

Since college wasn't mandatory in my family, I didn't have a perspective on it. When I started college, I was nervous. It was a new area for new friends, new people. I had no clue what I would need to do and learn. After graduation, I planned to get a job right away and get married, which I did.

As of now, I work for a doctor's office. A group of seventeen doctors. I work at home as an operator. I set their schedules and do interviews for colonoscopies and do medical-history-related tasks.

THE GREY AREA

My definition of the grey area is not knowing what's next, not having any plans. I never thought about the grey area. It can be a regrettable emotional state when deciding because you are unsure of what you are doing. It can be horrifying not knowing what's next and what's around the corner. I haven't had an extended period of a grey area in my life. I've always known what I've wanted, keep going day to day, what I need to do, and just do it.

HAPPENSTANCE? FATE? OR BOTH?

Well, I believe God has our plans in a destination for us, so we are given a choice to decide what we want to go with and the decisions we need to make. I believe things just seem to happen, whether we choose what we made or God's design and plan. I don't know. But I believe that things just happen. So I think fate. I don't know if it's real fate. I believe more in God's destiny for us to do things, to be a certain way, to do a certain thing. To be with certain people.

COLLEGE IS…

It is a little different for me because I didn't go away to college. I stayed at home and drove to downtown Dayton every day. Now

I look at college as furthering your education, preparing your life for the next step.

I think attending college is very important. College is a lot different from when I went to college. College is a lot more serious than before. You learned a lot more things from when I went to college. I feel I breezed through college, but when I look at my kids and the things they are going through, I know it's a lot more complicated than when I attended.

When it comes to college, I would have done things differently if I had known back then what I know now. I would have probably gone into something a little bit better, a field that would have made more money. I don't know if I'd gone with the nursing career. I think I probably would have gone into pharmaceuticals. Pharmaceuticals offer a promising salary, a lot more than I would ever make being a medical assistant.

MY PHILOSOPHY

Lessons I cherish from college I'd tell someone else: Don't hurry up and get married. I think it's good to go away to college; I think it would have been better for me if I had gone away.

Francis

CEDARVILLE UNIVERSITY '16, B.S. MECHANICAL ENGINEERING

HOMETOWN: BROOKEVILLE, OH

AGE GROUP: 20s

Life Motto: *"Learn from other people's mistakes. You won't live long enough to make them all yourself."*

LIFE BEFORE COLLEGE

Like most people, I grew up learning from my parents. Learning habits I wanted to pick up and not pick up from them. I got instructions for general life early. I was ready to learn and take away more from other mentors in my life. I learned a lot from people I respected.

So I would say that played a big part in my upbringing; I saw their mistakes and tried to avoid them. But also, seeing from a unique perspective, I learned from my parents' mistakes and successes what I wanted to do and did not want to do.

I'm a somewhat boring person. So I don't think I ever had a dream of my own. I guess I wanted to be whomever I was admiring most at the time, in a sense. I remember a conversation with my dad where I said I wanted to be an electrician because he was an electrician. Then I tried to be a pastor because there was a pastor. I respected them a lot, and he was there for me a lot. Then Jimmy (the pastor) came in and said, "Listen, we have enough pastors; not everyone is going to be a pastor. So be who you can be, and if you want to serve in the church, serve in the church on the side."

COLLEGE OR NAH?

Because of the subconscious social pressure, I went to college. If you want success, go to college. I also have grown up with the idea from my parents and other people that I was too smart not to go to college.

Going into my senior year of high school, I sat down and thought, *All right, what am I good at?* If I figure out what I am good at, then maybe I can figure out a job. I thought to myself, I'm good at erasing doubt, and I'm good at math; I'll just be an engineer. What kind of engineer? Well, I'm crappy at chemicals, I don't like plastic, I can't understand electricity, and I suck at computers, so that leaves me mechanical. Go to college for that. So I went.

I am very analytical, so I'm not good with emotions or whatnot. I don't remember how I felt when I started college. For me, shifting into something like that is just a shift. So I didn't process the difference between going to high school versus going to college.

As far as the actual college experience, I felt overwhelmed a bit because I realized I was unprepared to live independently.

THE GREY AREA

Have you ever gone on a walk in a nature park with trails marked out? Sometimes you go in, and you want to find where the waterfall is. Then you end up on the wrong path, and you never see the waterfall.

There is a nature center up in Troy where I went several times with my girlfriend, and we were always trying to find the waterfall. We went six times, and we could never find the stupid thing. We took different trails, and we thought we were on the map every time, but we always ended up in the wrong part of the park.

That's how I would describe the grey area. It's more of figuring out what path you want to take; No one knows their journey, but people know where they want to end up. The unknown is the path they will take to get to their known destination.

I would say the grey area is permanent for most people because many people have an idea of what they want to do, and because they have never done it, they don't know if it's what they expect it to be.

For instance, people get into relationships, and it doesn't turn out how they wanted it to, and they end up miserable because they had this expectation that was so far different from the reality that they were irreconcilable in the end. The same thing happens with people getting their dream jobs then being miserable because their boss is a jerk.

Therefore, I think everyone is going to be in the grey area to some extent for most of his or her life; dissatisfaction is a part of the human experience to some extent. Not saying that some people can never be happy with anything, but tomorrow they think they could have something better.

HAPPENSTANCE? FATE? OR BOTH?

As a Christian, I believe God knows everything that's going to happen, but I don't believe He is up there planning everything we are going to do. The analogy I use most is chess. The way I think of it, this is again assuming that God exists; I think of Him more than a grandmaster in chess playing a five-year-old. A five-year-old can do whatever move he wants. Sometimes, people do things on a whim, but playing against an opponent, being God who reacts, the grandmaster wins chess. The five-year-old never wins. Just doesn't happen, but the way the board looks at the end is entirely up to how the five-year-old plays. So, I would say I believe in the entire incident, but certain things are bound to happen. How they end up happening is entirely up to the individuals.

#GOALS

My plan for college was predetermined for me. Because I attended a slightly smaller school, many of the engineering courses are only offered one semester, and you need them for the next year as the same semester course. So they handed me a schedule; You'll take this block of classes this semester, this block of classes next semester through all four years and fit these many electives into it. So I had a literal four-year plan, and that's what I was doing. I had college credits going into it, but I had a literal four-year plan.

POST COLLEGE

Post-college was a bit of anxiety because I didn't have a job lined up immediately after graduating. Now, looking back on college, I miss it in a sense; I miss the camaraderie that exists when you live and work with people 24/7.

As of now, I'm working as an engineer at the University of Dayton Research Institute. My technical title is the associate's research engineer. If you care that much, I don't personally. I work there, but I want to volunteer at my church's high school and youth group. I do a class for high schoolers. Most of what I do is with them; I use engineering to help with that through them.

COLLEGE IS...

I would say college is a place to prepare people for technical jobs that wouldn't be cost-effective for their employees to teach them on the job. For instance, my job with engineering wouldn't make sense for my employer to sit down and teach me all about stress and all that stuff. It wouldn't make sense because they would have to sit down with me for years teaching me before I had enough background knowledge to begin my job. So I would say the purpose of college is to teach people to do jobs that require a background of extensive knowledge.

I see college as an excellent tool for people going into a field that can make enough money to pay for it. Some people will pay for it through scholarships, but if your job is in high enough demand that it could pay for your student loans, then college is a tool for you to earn money. If you are planning on going into a not high-paying field that is just enough for you to live on, then I don't see why a college would be necessary for such a lifestyle. Because in my opinion, college should pay for itself over time, if not immediately then soon after. But I had to go to college; I know people who majored in drama or music paid for a four-year degree at a $30,000 college school each year. I don't see a major in drama as a wise investment.

    I am satisfied with my degree in some sense. I wish I had learned more about programming to go into a slightly different field. But I'm content with where I am. I'm satisfied because I don't see my current job as my primary job or thing I do.

MY PHILOSOPHY

For people going to college, sit down and evaluate what you want to do with what kind of degree. If you don't know what you want to do, you take general education classes at a community college. It is better to have internships and learn other small things to understand what you want to do because college is not a place where you figure out what you want to do. It's preparing people that know what they already want to do. So I would say I don't go to a specialized college to take general education. Don't pick a college because someone you know is going there because people break up. Go in with a direction because if you go in with a direction, you pay a lot of money per day to not know what you are doing.

Gabriel

B.S. Central State University '91
B.S. University of Dayton '95
M.S.Ed University of Dayton '03
Ed.S. University of Dayton '05
Hometown: Dayton, OH
Age Group: 50s

Life Motto: *"If you have some who are caught up in the fault, like brethren, those who are caught up in the fault, restore that person with the spear of meekness, lest you also get caught up in that."* What comes down in life is based upon relationships. I look at my relationship with God because of how God has treated me. That's how I want to treat others. That's come through life learning; that's not a perspective I had before, even when people do things wrong. In relationships, you are gonna get hurt sometimes; in that piece, do you want to reach back the same way? That's the natural reaction. You want to try to restore people; life is based on relationships. Your relationship with Christ determines your relationship with everybody else.

LIFE BEFORE COLLEGE

There are a lot of different factors about what shaped my upbringing. Having friends and family and so many who are so different impacts you significantly. You see some good things that you pick up, and then you see some things and think, *I don't want to climb up that type of tree.* So there are some positives, and there are some negatives with that. But ultimately, I would say pretty much what I did was my own choice, and the other part of that is it makes you who you are.

During adolescence, I thought I wanted to be an electrician at first. I was in high school at the time, and my high school was a well-known vocational school. So I enrolled with plans to be an electrician, but when I got there, they changed the program to what was known as digital electronics because computers were going to be the future.

Believe it or not, for me, I wasn't interested in learning about computers. I remember we learned about electrical boards and stuff like that, but then when we learned to program for a binary number and everything, I had no interest in that stuff. Thus, it was not what I came to this program for. I came to be an electrician, not to study digital electronics.

COLLEGE OR NAH?

Before my college experience, I had no plans whatsoever. When people first talked about college, I was like, "Nope, I'm not going to college. People in college are poor; they get nothing." My band director was very influential and knew I needed to go to college.

He knew I enjoyed playing music, so he told me I could go to college on a music scholarship. He took me under his wing, and I could go to college and have a partial music scholarship.

I didn't have any real perspective of college at the time. During my childhood, college was not even in my vocabulary. We would go down and perform at parades at Alabama State University; that was my first time even paying attention to any type of college.

When beginning college, I had a different mindset because I was all about music. So going to an HBCU, the band was a big thing; you noticed people didn't pay too much attention to the football team. People were paying attention to the band. My goal was to be a section leader as a drummer. The college I attended had a strong music program. I had never seen people perform like that before. I had some great instructors who were so gifted; that was an eye-opener for me. So I had a lot of fun learning music.

THE GREY AREA

For me, the grey area has to do with what I thought I wanted to do and wanted to become, and things changed. I thought my goal was to be a music teacher. So I started out going to college as a music education major. Many music education majors were there for at least five years, and my undergrad was only supposed to be four years. I remember walking around campus one day trying to figure out what I was going to do because I didn't want to be there for five years. I walked around campus trying to figure out what I would major in because I had decided that I would no longer major in music. So that was a pretty grey area for me at the time.

At this point and time, I would say I'm not in the grey area because I've been doing what I wanted to do for the past 25 years. So that part's not a grey area, but deciding the next step phase of my life could be a grey area. Trying to determine what I should do next. Where can I improve? Where can I help?

HAPPENSTANCE? FATE? OR BOTH?

I believe everything has already been predestined.

#GOALS

My so-called four-year plan for college was to graduate in four years. I knew college was supposed to be four years, so when I started majoring in music and seeing the music education majors had many music classes you had to take, I got discouraged. When I mapped it out with my advisor and kept looking back at it, I realized it would take me over four years. They didn't have a program instilled where you can graduate in four years. I was almost tempted to go ahead and join the army, but my granny didn't like that idea.

POST COLLEGE

I was the first college graduate out of the family. So that was a massive thing for me, mainly because I thought I would never go to college. I remembered we celebrated the night before graduation.

I knew where I was going. I had a great mentor. I applied to several colleges, got accepted to two at the time, went to the experimental psychology program, and had a full scholarship. Everything was paid for, even though it was out of state. So that was kind of my post-grad plan, but of course, I didn't finish that program there.

Somebody I met there, a graduate from the central state back in 1968, asked if I had ever thought about being a counselor, and I said no. He was a counselor. He said, "Have you ever thought about going to the University of Dayton (UD) and pursuing their counseling program?" I told him no, I'm not going to UD. I had my biases about UD at the time. But, low and behold, I ended up studying the counseling program at UD and eventually ended up doing the school psychology program there and have not looked back since. It was a significant experience, better than what I ever anticipated.

Right now, I'm working as a special education supervisor. My background is as a school psychologist, as well as research at the university.

COLLEGE IS...

A place you will learn and acquire book knowledge and establish relationships that will greatly impact the rest of your life. The college experience is unique. I would say college can be some of the best years of your life. I remember when I had my first physical to go to college, and my family doctor at the time said, "Your college years are going to be some of the best years of your life." I didn't have a clue what he was talking about at the time. But for me, my experience with the band and all that other stuff indeed were great. I have some relationships that I still enjoy today. I met my wife there, never thought I would have met my spouse in college. So it was a good experience. Of course, you go through some challenges as well, but overall the experiences were pretty good.

Was it worth the debt? I think if I would have been more knowledgeable or if somebody said, "Hey man, you know you have to pay all this back," I think I would have looked at some other options. I'm quick to share with people that college isn't for everybody. But, unfortunately, a lot of people believe college is the only way to go. If my advisor during high school would've aligned me to make a trade, I would have.

I think I would've had a different life. Meaning, sure enough, I wouldn't have incurred this much debt just to learn a trade. You can always look at a trade, you can go in, go do your training for a year or so, get an apprenticeship, and from there, you are out making your living. Don't have any debt behind you or other stuff. I see it in two ways; I will always encourage anybody to get as much education as they can. Just keep it in perspective. Know that a college degree can set you up for a great job. People who have college degrees pursued their degrees to stand out in the job market and go to have a higher standard of living. People can make a living and haven't had a day in college. Your degree is something to hold your head up and be proud of...and you can use it to help you move forward.

In the grand scheme of things, I am satisfied with my degree. I am grateful for what God has provided. I'm most grateful definitely for the support I received from family as well as the encouragement. It's something I had never envisioned. I never anticipated getting a degree; I never expected to have multiple degrees. So when I say earning a degree is something that was not in my plan, earning a degree was not in my plan.

M'KAI FOLLEY

MY PHILOSOPHY

Become knowledgeable about your student loans, become knowledgeable about what your debt is going to look like. Don't let debt deter you, but have a realistic picture of what it will look like. If I had to do that part back over, that would be the most significant piece. I would look more into how much college is going to cost; weigh my pros and cons. Keep it in perspective. Don't let debt deter you because it can deter you, but have a realistic perspective about what things will look like.

Lori-Ann "LA" Stacey

Tufts University '14, B.A. English and
Women's Gender & Sexuality Studies

Teachers College, Columbia University '18,
M.A. Sociology and Education Policy

Hometown: Mt. Vernon, N.Y.

Age Group: 20s

Life Motto: *"I had one from Lil Wayne, "love, live life, proceed, progress," and it's corny as hell to say that, but I stand by that."*

LIFE BEFORE COLLEGE

My family is originally from Jamaica; both my mom and dad are from Montego Bay. I grew up in a small city outside of the Bronx, Mt. Vernon, NY. I would describe my upbringing as very typical for a Caribbean immigrant home. On Sundays, we had Jamaican breakfast - ackee and saltfish, plantain, callaloo - and my mom cleaned. To be honest, looking back, it was fascinating to me that I was not cleaning like other children. I remember the music being on and cleaning my room. However, I never cleaned the bathroom or the kitchen or any major areas. My mom let me off easy with only *sometimes* cleaning the living room, which was never messy.

There were always expectations instilled, as far as educational attainment and college. Not attending college was never an option. That understanding hit me the hardest in middle school. I remember my friends and me getting ready to go to high school and thinking about the next steps. In 7th grade, I applied to a boarding school in Westchester, but I was told only accepted for their day school due to proximity. That wasn't feasible in terms of transportation and the hours my mom worked. I entered 8th-grade content because I would go to Mt. Vernon High School, with my friends.

Unfortunately, MVHS didn't have the best reputation. My mom sat me down and said something to the effect of, "Absolutely not!" She made it clear that I was smart enough and talented enough to get into these programs, which I did, and the rest she would figure out. Trust and believe I was not going to Mt. Vernon High School, and she squashed any fantasies or defeatist attitudes I had about it.

I got lucky. A big part of my upbringing was that my mom always wanted more from an immigrant mentality for me. She often said, "I came here so you can have the best, and I'm going to work hard so you can have that." I know we weren't the most well off family, but I always felt good. She always made sure of that.

Eventually, I applied for the National A Better Chance program and was accepted to their community boarding program. I went to school in Guilford, Connecticut, about 20-30 minutes outside of New Haven. It was a very drastic shift. At the time, I really thought I was doing this for my mom - she came to the United

States so I could have the best education, which was rooted firmly in her Jamaican ideals. But, it was always for me and even after everything, I would do it again.

As a first-generation citizen, I experienced a tension between my Jamaican roots and my American identity. I always knew I was Black; I know my family is from Jamaica, but I didn't grow up feeling comfortable embracing my Jamaican identity outside of my friends and family. Part of this was my mom's constant reminder to my brother and me that we weren't born in Jamaica and, therefore, not Jamaican. She insisted we were American. This tension between citizenship and culture was apparent in her need to ensure that we always knew we belonged. For me, it had the opposite effect. I always felt a little bit bothered. Not Jamaican enough, or not American enough.

As an adolescent, I was planning on being a pediatrician. That was my dream since I was seven. *I want to be a doctor; I want to be a pediatrician.* That was my constant refrain until I got to college. I was always good at math, and I grew curious about the sciences - both came naturally to me, and so it made sense to pursue medicine as I progressed in school. At the same time, I also really loved writing. It was a way to be creative, but I never allowed myself to explore it beyond that. That quiet exploration influenced me when I got to college.

Attending a community boarding program at a predominately white high school in a predominately white town shifted a lot of my experiences with the school. (We all know the studies on Black girls being pushed out of STEM - Google it). I grew up with teachers that looked like me - Black or Jamaican - and lived in my neighborhood. They encouraged me, "Lori, you are a smart girl."

They pushed me and challenged me in math. I was always one of the best students, and this was an inherent belief that was part of my identity. High school was the first time I didn't have supportive teachers, as I did in middle and elementary school.

When I attended high school, I was still good at school, but that level of support no longer existed. I had White teachers. I had racist teachers. I had teachers who did not care. Math went from being a subject I loved to one I didn't care for. My freshman year was the first time I had a terrible math teacher. I did well, but there was no joy.

My experience in high school, not having adults pour into me, was probably when I started to skirt through things. I realized I didn't have to try as hard to do well, especially since no one was pushing me to go above my capabilities. For example, I had a double period science class freshman year, where I slept through the first half of the class. I would wake up to do the labs and get A's on the test. The other students would tell me directly, "That's ridiculous, it doesn't even make sense," and the teacher would complain to my guidance counselor or whoever she could. It wasn't that I was not interested in the subject; I was bored. I wasn't being challenged, and the end goal was to be able to do the work, not to think critically or achieve beyond measure. I wish I knew better then, but I didn't, so I slept.

COLLEGE OR NAH?

I was always going to go to college. It was always the expectation. College was spoken about in the same way that high school was. It was the next step, so going to college never felt like a choice.

I was absolutely ready to attend college. My senior year of high school was tough, and I was ready to say "Peace out!" to Mt. Vernon and Guilford. Tufts University was always my number one choice. There was a brief period where I thought *maybe I'd go to Columbia*. I applied Early-Decision to Columbia and got deferred. I'm a very dramatic person, and I asked them to remove me from the applicant pool, so I guess I'll never know if I would have gotten in. (Spoiler - I got in for my graduate degree). I immediately applied Early-Decision Round 2 to Tufts, and it was the best decision ever.

I was excited. I did a pre-orientation program, mostly so I could be on campus early and because I wanted to choose my bed first. Everyone who came to school early was ready for the journey to begin. I wasn't even thinking about classes. I was more preoccupied with the social part of college. In those first few weeks, walking around and being on my own, I would think, '*This* is what people talk about.'

My whole life - elementary school, middle school, high school—everyone talked about college, college, college, and more college. Which might be the problem. The focus is you just need to get to college. No one talks about your life after college. Then here I was, I got there. *Now what?*

THE GREY AREA

The grey area, for me, is the tension that exists between expectations of childhood and the reality of adulthood. When we are younger, there is immense pressure to figure out what we want to do in life, what we want to be, or what career path we will pursue. We talk to children about all of 10 careers, and these lead to expectations and even goals for our future. It can be hard to wrestle with the idea that the visions we had of ourselves aren't necessarily coming true.

It's hard to describe. The grey area feels like a space of not knowing even when there is a clear path, even when you are working toward your goals. For instance, the classes you take, the volunteering, the networking, and the people you meet lead towards an end goal. You might have a clear idea in your head what that is, but the grey area is the wiggle room that surrounds that. You might have an end goal in mind as you put in all this time and effort, but no one can predict the future, so you don't *really* know the end goal.

I have a ten-year plan. It may come to fruition; it may not. But in 10 years, when I look back, I'll be able to say, "Wow, all of this was leading up to where I am now." That's the grey area - the unknown, the unplanned, the changes in direction that all feels like a mish-mosh of grey and globs of whites and blacks. While I'm in the grey area, I can imagine, I can envision, but I can't *see* the result. There is a sense that you have to remove yourself and be in a reflective state to truly be clear.

At this moment, I would say I'm in the latter half of the grey area. It's becoming more black and white. When I first graduated from Tufts, I was in the grey area because I didn't know what I wanted to do. I convinced myself I'd get my masters in social work and pursue social work as a career. While at Tufts, having pivoted from pre-med, I interned at a domestic violence center and with a domestic violence legal aid organization. At the time, social work made the most sense. But I was completely unsure. As much as I thought about that, I created a plan to go to law school. My internships influenced this, and I thought I could play a more vital role with a law degree. I remember one day during that first summer, I sat down at my kitchen table, and I read three pages of the LSAT study guide. After about 30 minutes, I was like, okay, I'm over it.

I decided to focus on applying to jobs. My list was all over the place. I was applying to be the program manager, director of things and not understanding that my bachelor's degree would not allow me to be in those kinds of roles yet. In the middle of not knowing what I wanted to do, I was also facing the harsh reality and misconception of college and what doors a bachelor's degree can open.

I just knew I needed a job. I ended up working as a resident counselor for a summer internship program, and I loved it! I love being around children and students. When I reflect, and this is what I mean about being removed, all my experiences - even when focused on pre-med or contemplating social work - were leading up to being a resident counselor and eventually education. When I truly think about my adolescence and wanting to be a pediatrician, my why was always rooted in supporting children to be healthy and be their best selves. It was about working with children who looked like me in my community and ensuring they had better.

Career-wise, I am in that part of the grey area where I know the industry I want to be in; I want to be an educator. It's something that's always been and will be a part of my life, and I've embraced that now. So in this grey, with partial black and white, I am figuring out what route to take within education.

I believe the grey area is temporary in that it's always shifting. There are times when the grey area surrounding your path feels like a cloudy day, and other times it's a heavy fog. We see differences in both, but the path is always there. We are constantly wading through the greyness in our lives. It's okay to not always know what lies ahead, as long as we're courageous enough to keep moving forward.

HAPPENSTANCE? FATE? OR BOTH?

I want to say both. I'm a firm believer that you end up where you are supposed to be. From day to day, that's hard to accept. Things may feel like a coincidence; the interactions may feel random. But ultimately, every person, place, or thing (yay, nouns) can be a lesson or a step on your journey. I like to believe that no matter how friendships, jobs, or opportunities work out in a moment - for the better or sometimes for the worse - it shapes a better path and future. You end up right where you're meant to be.

#GOALS

Did I have a four-year plan? Yes and no. Tufts reaches out to low-income, historically underserved students interested in the sciences and conducts a pre-assessment. So I already knew what lay ahead for pre-med. They helped build out my schedule and gave me an idea of what the next four years would look like if I stuck to pre-med. Academically, I had a rough draft starting out pre-med.

In high school, I expected to attend medical school right after college. I never thought I'd be working upon graduation. Tufts also had a program where you could do accelerated coursework and guarantee acceptance into medical school at the end of junior year. Obviously, that did not happen for me. The goals I had entering college are not the same goals I am pursuing now.

POST COLLEGE

After college graduation, I kept thinking *I'm not going to get a job. Why did I choose to be an English/Women Studies major? I need to go back to school. I don't want to take the GRE.* I had a lot of anxiety about what the next steps were. I was resigned to take anything that would come my way.

I was looking at master's programs in social work. I was looking at law programs. I was trying to avoid tests and kept researching which programs don't require the GRE or the LSAT? I was all over the place and applying for jobs at random. I felt hopeless and lost, and while I kept making a joke out of it, I thought I'd never get a job I was passionate about.

Now that I have my masters, this time around, the job hunt is a lot better. I have more clarity and focus. I understand what my degree qualifies me for and where I can be firm in what I want out of a job and a career. I'm also a lot more patient with myself. To buy time over the summer, I worked as an Associate Director for the same summer internship program I did after Tufts.

I know what I deserve. I refuse to put myself in a position where I'm accepting less than I deserve, especially as a Black woman. We are already overeducated and underpaid. My focus is not settling for roles just because I'm feeling anxious or getting desperate for a job. That's the hardest part right now.

At the point of this conversation, I am unemployed. I'm using this time to interview for jobs. Looking back, I will say I did not think it would be this hard to find a job. Throughout your academic career, the focus is to get to college, get your bachelors, and get a job. I did that, and yet here I am; why can't I find a job? I spent 3 months after Tufts searching, and now, even with my masters, I have received low offers or told I don't have enough experience for the positions I am excited about. I'm better off in the job hunt now than before. When I graduated from Tufts, I did not understand; it was not adding up. I felt bamboozled.

COLLEGE IS....

When I look back at college, I feel like it was a valuable experience. I love the friends that I made. I like some of the classes I took. I appreciate the opportunities I had. I didn't network as much with professors as I should have, but I developed a great relationship with my dean.

I went into college slightly naive, believing it would be what I saw on TV. In some ways, it was, and in some ways, it was not. I played rugby freshman year, I was on the step team, I was president of the Caribbean club, I studied abroad for a year, and I traveled throughout Europe. I also almost failed a math course, could not get about a B in Spanish and quit internships. While I learned a lot about myself - through the ups and the downs - I thought my learning and aspirations would be concrete by the time I left, and if you've made it this far, you know that it wasn't

The reality is that college is an institution. The institution cares more about what you can contribute than what you can gain. It's not solely your tuition; as alumni, there is donating, attending events, supporting recruitment etc. The focus for colleges is about upholding institutions and institutional values rather than student success. It's why students should contemplate and choose a college wisely.

As a Black woman, I encourage other Black women to deeply consider what they want to gain from their college experience. Your institution will be demanding labor, time, resources, energy, and finances. You need to be poised to meet those demands and take as much as you can during your time. There are wonderful opportunities to grow outside of the classroom and the realities to be faced.

You learn a lot about the social order through your campus interactions especially along various demographics including race, gender, class, etc. As great as it can be, there are also some harsh realities to face about your peers and what they have been conditioned to expect from college and you as a Black woman. You learn about your professors' viewpoints and perspectives. You learn about whiteness, racism, sexism, and the pervasiveness amongst progressive movements. You learn a lot.

College is a microcosm of the real world. Sometimes the most valuable lessons will be how to navigate these social interactions. While college recruiting focuses on academics and extracurriculars, the reality is that people will graduate in worse academic standings and still have better outcomes because of their social standings. Networking is as real as people make it out to be. Have fun and navigate strategically.

MY PHILOSOPHY

College is what you make it. If you want the quintessential college experience, then make it that. Go to the open houses for the obscure clubs, run for student government, learn a new sport, study abroad, skip class to go to a concert, party on a Wednesday, Thursday and a Monday - if that's what you want to do.

Success will ultimately look the way you want it to. Some people skated through college and now work for their parents, or Google, or Apple, and there are others who were at the top of their program pursuing PhDs. There are so many options in between, but you have to follow your gut and make the decisions that benefit you. What is meant for you will always be yours and will find a way to be yours. At the time of this publication, I can say I am truly happy with all (okay, most) of my decisions.

I did all the dumb things (but not illegal). I participated in my school's naked quad run, I went to clubs, I cut my hair, I danced on tables, and one time I even pre-gamed while trying to submit my final paper. Have fun and stay focused.

As much as college is about academics and the next steps in life - you have your entire life to work. You have your entire life to make your dreams come true. You will graduate, find a job, build your 401K, buy a house, and do all the other things you want to do. So embrace those 4 years as a time to learn about yourself and say yes to more adventures and first times. It's okay to explore different friendship groups and meet new people. The friends that you meet freshman year may be your friends in senior year or not. Find different people to study with, laugh with, party with, and go on new adventures with.

Do everything. It's easy to forget that we are children at that age. I was a child at 18 years old. I did not know the world; I thought I knew it, though. I had a lot of experience adjusting to and acclimating to different environments, but I did not know the world. You don't want to look back and think, *Wow, I studied too much* and *Wow, I never tried out for this team.* My advice for myself at that age and anyone else would be to try new things, don't hold yourself back, and be yourself.

Do more, be more, and see more.

Mari

B.S. in Mathematics

Age Group: 40s

Life Motto: *"Golden rule. Be kind to other people. Don't be an asshole. It doesn't mean you have to be amazingly nice to everybody. Just don't be a jerk."*

LIFE BEFORE COLLEGE

My parents were very supportive of my goals, which is excellent and a little scary. My parents' support gave me a great platform to try things and I knew whatever I did was okay.

So many things shaped my mindset growing up in New York City. Coming from a mixed family background molded me where I am now because I always have tried to see both sides of everything. Some of that was just because of my ethnic background, and some of it was what my parents encouraged me to do in general. I try to look at things from different perspectives; obviously, I have my opinions about things. Still, I try to understand what other people are thinking from different perspectives.

My upbringing has had both a personal and business impact on my life. I would even say it's helped me as a person who does project management for software development. My upbringing makes me think about what kinds of questions other people will ask, and that's not something that I was taught in school.

I didn't necessarily have a specific dream as a kid. In high school, I wanted to be an environmental science major in college. I tried to save the world. I had this very nebulous idea of what that meant. I knew I wanted to be involved and serve the community somehow. I thought I was going to be a biologist or something and research animals.

COLLEGE OR NAH?

It was understood I would go to college. I wouldn't say college was mandatory. If I could have made a case to my parents that I didn't want to go, they would have been okay with it. But it wasn't a conversation we ever had. It wasn't negative, either. Everyone in our family has gone to college. If I said, "I want to go to a trade school," my parents would have been okay with my decision.

I'm not sure I had any preconceived notions of college. I assumed as a kid that college was a school you went to when you were older.

I was overwhelmed and was feeling nervous when I started college because I am an only child. I never had to share a room with anybody. So I had no idea what that was going to be like.

The reality was my high school prepared me well; I was overly prepared compared to a lot of people. I wasn't worried about the amount of work, which I found surprising. I did more work in my senior year of high school than in college.

THE GREY AREA

I'm in the grey area right now. I relate the grey area to the idea of not being sure what's next. Not necessarily thinking, *Oh my god, what I am doing is wrong.* Maybe I evolved out of what I'm doing. There is the next step, and I'm not sure what the next step is.

I have been at my job now with the government for over ten years. I've been doing some of the same things since I started. So, I mean, let's just face it, it's a little boring. It's not that I don't like my job; I'm just not challenged anymore. On the other hand, I was challenged to a degree with this project last year, which reinvigorated me a little.

At this point, I'm not thinking about retirement, but I am thinking about what's next. I've been at my job for a long time. I want to do things, and I'm not sure how to incorporate them into what I do right now.

I've gotten very involved in supporting women in tech and advocating for women in tech; that is fundamental to me. I'm trying to figure out how to incorporate more of that into my career. Within the last two years, I started a business where I'm coaching women in tech and realized I loved coaching. It's whirled into me doing speaking engagements about women and diversity. I'm heading toward something, and I don't know what it is.

The grey area describes where I am right now. I do not want to necessarily quit my job because I do like my job. There are some frustrating things, of course, but that's with any job. But I also got all these other pieces, and I'm trying to figure out how exactly they connect.

Then there's the piece that I could potentially retire in ten years, and what does that mean? I don't imagine I'll stop working, but what would I be doing?

I think we will always have grey areas. Life is dynamic. I think you might be in a grey area of one sort for a while, and then you move on and end up in another grey area for different reasons. Then you are maybe there for a little bit of time and then you are not.

HAPPENSTANCE? FATE? OR BOTH?

I believe in happenstance. Do I believe in fate? I'm not sure. I guess I believe in some parts of all of those things. Sometimes things just happen, and I think you can be in the right place at the right time or the wrong place at the wrong time. I believe that sometimes a bad thing probably should have happened in my life, but it didn't. Either I put myself in a situation that wasn't safe, or whatever. Some things happen you cannot explain. I think to some degree, we unintentionally control things. For instance, we make choices that direct us and guide us. We don't necessarily know that we have done it, so it seems that it's the end. We make choices, and we aren't necessarily making choices with a focus on a particular goal.

#GOALS

I planned to graduate with a degree in biology and go save the world. I had no plan other than that. I was going to graduate, get a job, and life was going to be great.

There's a saying that goes, *You can look at the landscape, and you can see as far as the edge of the cliff, and then everything after that is grey.*

I could see the end of school, I could see myself graduating, but then everything else after that—I had no idea. Not a clue!

POST COLLEGE

Leading up to graduation, I was excited. It was a milestone in my life. *I am done! I don't have to do work anymore*—however, reality sets in pretty quickly. I ended up moving across the country right after college. I graduated, and I left the following Monday. I had no idea what job I was going to do. I ended up getting a recommendation and finding a job; it all worked out. But! There were a lot of wings and prayers.

Currently, I am working as an analyst in the District of Columbia in a tech agency. I have my own business as a life and wellness coach. I am a yoga instructor as well. I'm going to be taking a little hiatus from actively instructing. I'm doing way too much right now. I mentioned I'm doing a lot of advocacy for women in tech, which happens to be part of my business and a very personal thing that I do. I organize happy hours and breakfast because it's about supporting people in terms of *Hey, here's how to get a new job* and supporting people in terms of *Hey, you have a community looking out for you.*

COLLEGE IS...

While college is a place where adults get an education, I think there is more to college than that. It's the first time many people are away from home, and it's a learning experience about life; you are still in this bubble of safety. You don't have to worry too much that you will get hurt or damaged somehow, but you can start exploring or dip your toes into the waters of adulthood.

College is a transition; you are still in the education bubble. But you are leading toward breaking out and moving into the world—the caterpillar's transformation to the butterfly.

College for me was an opportunity to not be at home. Not having the restriction and the safety of home. I had to make choices, and I couldn't always fall back on my parents for those choices.

Overall, college was an excellent experience for me. I'm glad I did it; I'm glad I went where I went. I think where I went had a lot of influence on how I feel about my college experience. I'm thrilled I went to a small school.

MY PHILOSOPHY

Nothing is guaranteed, which, unfortunately, students are not taught. The thing that comes to mind foremost, both positive and negative: You are not assured of a place anywhere. You can do many things to get yourself in a position, so you might get what you are reaching towards. But it is not certain you will.

Isaac

HOWARD UNIVERSITY '16, B.A. POLITICAL SCIENCE
w/ CONCENTRATION IN CHEMISTRY
COLUMBIA UNIVERSITY '17, MPA IN
ENVIRONMENTAL SCIENCE AND POLICY
HOMETOWN: PLAINFIELD, NJ
AGE GROUP: 20s

Life Motto: *"Anything is possible."*

LIFE BEFORE COLLEGE

Both of my parents are very spiritual, and that shaped my upbringing. Growing up in the community plays a vital role in my life, who I am and what I do. My mom and dad were always involved in the community, and I took the key to that. When I was younger, I was interested in politics and I was a member of the student government at my school. I also wanted to be a singer, a writer, and work in medicine.

Mad shootings were happening in our community when I was in high school, and my friends wanted to do something about it. I remember one of my friends invited me to this meeting. She said, "We are trying to change the city, and it's gonna be huge." I told my other two friends to come, and they came. We all ended up becoming close friends.

We started a nonprofit, being a voice for youth in the community, and loved the impact and power. As a child, you are fearless, and as you get older, you get more paranoid and concerned about negative people poisoning your mind.

I loved the energy, the drive, and the push. We had an impact we could make on our community.

Today, I think I'm diverging back into politics oddly enough; I don't know how. I was accepted by Howard as a chemistry major. I wanted to be, and still aspire, to be a doctor. However, I changed my major sophomore year because medicine did not arouse me as politics did; politics in DC inspired me. Watching how people change like chameleons is interesting.

COLLEGE OR NAH?

Why did I go to college? To get away from home. I'm serious! I knew I wanted to go to college. I needed to leave because things at home were just getting out of control. My dad and I weren't seeing eye to eye at all. It was very confrontational. My home was a dreary place for me. I just needed to get out, and if I could prove to myself, I could get out and create freedom for myself—*Let me do that*. That was the fundamental drive to go to college. Yes, education and stuff, but that's coupled with freedom.

College was an unspoken word in my family. It was more so like, "Yeah, you need to go to college." When I first started, I was scared. I thought I was not going to make friends and be an outcast. For the first two months, I wanted to leave Howard. I didn't feel like I fit in because many people were going to parties and doing all that type of crazy mess, and I wasn't.

I knew a good friend who was the team leader for our freshman seminar group, and he never showed up to one meeting! Finally, he showed up at the last one, and we ended up becoming friends. It's just crazy how life works out.

Although I was scared, I was excited and anxious to see what college had for me. The truth is, nobody is ever prepared to go to college.

THE GREY AREA

The grey area exists because society puts this expectation that this is what you are supposed to do. Who are you supposed to please? Who are you listening to? Are you listening to the right people? Are you listening to yourself?

It can be powerful once you come out of your grey area and have solace and confirmation of steadfastness in what you discover out of your grey area. The grey area is a limbo and while in limbo you are trying to find direction for your life. Moreover, the grey area is a lost place in the middle of something great.

Your grey area is supposed to be your space for you to figure out what you are supposed to do—so don't allow too many people to get into your area. Sometimes people put too many people in their grey area, making it so hard for them to try and decide for themselves what they are supposed to be doing with their lives and who they are supposed to be.

I'm starting to get out of my grey area. Though, I feel I've got to cut a few more strings from my old self to allow myself to get out of my grey area. Throughout life, as you grow, you are going to have multiple seasons with different grey areas. You are always evolving; you are always getting better or bigger; you should be.

HAPPENSTANCE? FATE? OR BOTH?

I believe in destiny. I feel certain situations are opposed to your purpose, and your destiny happens. Your destiny is already written. Depending on how much you push your faith and yourself, you can expand the fate written for you and use what God is giving you. In life, some coincidences don't have a long-lasting impact. It's usually the ones you think are minuscule that leaves an imprint on your life.

I think we make destiny harder by being hard-headed and not listening, but God will turn a misstep or a critical step into something that puts you right back on your path. You can have additional steps in your life, but there is no step to reverse your fate because it's already written for you.

#GOALS

My four-year plan was to go to medical school post-college graduation. In college, I considered joining a fraternity, but I didn't. I wanted to be valedictorian, too. I was going to get into medical school and be debt-free. Going debt-free was a big thing for me.

POST COLLEGE

My thoughts after I graduated was the song, *"I feel like a man when I walk through!"* I felt I accomplished something because I got into grad school and had a bulk of it paid for. I was out here winning.

My pre-college plans changed from my post-college plans. I went to grad school, and after that, became a planner. I had the perfect idea to come to LA to get the ideal job. I told myself, *I have friends out here, I'm gonna get a car, and I'm gonna finally be stable for once in my life. That way, I can work on other parts of my life.* Once I got to LA, I thought, *I'm just going to be in* an *oasis of peace…* but that was not my reality.

I came out to LA, and instead of doing something I want to do, I'm working at a non-profit that's combating climate change through a market-based system. Rich people can purchase expensive projects to reduce emissions and sell them back to make more money. They are helping the environment, but I feel the benefits are not going to the people who need them.

I'm also an actor. I finished this film program with Nate Parker. It was a learning experience for me. I came in with a set of plans to attack something and it went differently.

COLLEGE IS…

College is an experience. First, I thought it was necessary to progress yourself in education, but college is more about discovering yourself. Once you discover yourself and learn how to work with people, the sky's the limit.

I realized college is more of a nesting ground, a training ground for life for everything, from relationships to classes, to finances.

Life changes; a one-minute event can change your entire path. Be willing to learn how to be versatile. Learn how to adjust yourself in certain circumstances.

If you can go to college, go to college because college is a great place for you to learn about yourself and the type of person you want to be. Life is crueler than college. In college, you are more shielded and protected, but college is a microcosm of life. It's the biggest thing to help you discover who you are, who you want to be.

MY PHILOSOPHY

Don't allow one 'no' to stop you from doing what you want to, even if it's your parents. Sometimes you have to listen to your inner voice and find people who can encourage that small voice inside to be louder. It's many people in the world; they'll tell you a lot of no's, they have a lot of fear. If you say, "I will not listen to that," if you have this hunger for your dreams, you can do that, you do that. Be serious when you are following your dreams. Are you going to live or let it die? Living means it's a little hard; dying means it's easy. Which one are you going to take for yourself?

Malcom

UNIVERSIDAD AUTONOMA DE GUERRERO '84, M.D.

HOMETOWN: BROOKLYN, NY

AGE GROUP: 50S

Life Motto: *"An old Cherokee is teaching his grandson about life. 'A fight is going on inside of me,' he says to the boy. 'It is a terrible fight, and it is between two wolves. One is evil: He is anger, envy, sorrow, regret, arrogance, self-pity, guilt, resentment, inferiority, lies, false pride, superiority, self-doubt, and ego.*

"The other side is good: He is joy, peace, love, hope, serenity, humility, kindness, benevolence, empathy, generosity, truth, compassion, and faith. This same fight is going on inside you AND inside every other person too.' The grandson thinks about it for a minute and then asks his grandfather, 'Which wolf will win?' The old chief replied, 'The one you feed.'"

LIFE BEFORE COLLEGE

I'm the oldest of six children, and my parents constantly drilled the concept of responsibility. I handled siblings; I handled myself. So every step and everything I did was influential; my siblings were influenced by what I said and what I did. I was always one of those people that was slightly influential in position. So the action of my behaviors was initially influential.

My parents, being immigrant-Caribbean, told me there are four things you can be as a young man: a doctor, lawyer, an engineer, or a priest. So those things drove my Kodak lens through high school and then college. I was going to be a doctor, but I was driven not by self-interest. My parents had expectations, and it was written to me.

I questioned, what did it mean to be a doctor? Was that the choice for me? When I was a freshman in undergrad, I took pre-med lower classes, but they were not necessarily intriguing. Then I found courses such as psychology and sociology, and I started thinking about the human element. Even Economy 101 was fascinating to me, much more than the sciences.

COLLEGE OR NAH?

I went to college because college was mandatory in my family. My perspective now regarding college is I think a lot of people are not appropriately prepared for college. You have people who say, "I'm going to college," then you have people who say, "Well, I'm not going to college because people never told me about it." I don't think we do a good job of actively communicating and preparing people for college.

Beginning college was okay because I had friends with me, and I could connect with people quickly. But I knew I was on a campus that was not friendly to people of color, and their biases were apparent. Especially being a pre-med major, they anticipated my friend with whom I went to high school , and I didn't belong in the pre-med club or the pre-med class. So all of those things were very transparent. If anything, that became a driving factor, but definitely, the racism was extremely transparent.

THE GREY AREA

First of all, early on, I never believed in coincidences. I believed things happened because they were supposed to happen. Or somewhere, we caused something to happen. It could be us, the human element; it could be our energy or our spirit; our ancestors or elders' energy or spirit can also cause things to happen. Now we just think it's a coincidence, or we think somehow it is a miracle. No, those things were supposed to happen. You just didn't know it. It was spoken for you; it was made for you; the world, the energy, the spirits, and the elders thought it was best for you. I believe there are stages of the grey area and you move from stage to stage.

HAPPENSTANCE? FATE? OR BOTH?

I don't believe I'm big into happenstance. Fate, I'm still dealing. I believe I have ancestors; I have spirits who are with me, who support me and look after me, my elders. I call on them. I share my plans with them in a way that makes me feel supported by them—here is what I'm doing; here are the steps I'm taking based on life experiences and my surroundings; who cares about me? I put it out there in the energy for you to support me, guide me, and create a path. Now, it doesn't mean it's going to happen just like the way I planned it, but I'm working toward the goal. I believe everything is in me, the surrounding energy, people that support me, love me on the way, and will help me get to where I'm supposed to go.

#GOALS

My four-year plan was simple: finish pre-med and go to medical school.

POST COLLEGE

I went straight to medical school, but I attended medical school at a different college because another barrier was created. There are only so many slots in medical school in the US. A thousand students come out of pre-med, and there are only 100 slots for medical school. So it's beyond what your MCAT score is and beyond what your GPA in undergrad is; there's an interview, and it could still be biased. So I went to school in Mexico, which was a whole other experience.

In med school I was deeper into the wormhole. I invested more emotionally and financially because I had student loans to pay for my housing and school. My entire life was based on loans. I was in medical school, in a different country, experiencing a different culture....I felt I was going deeper into a wormhole.

My post-college timeline changed because I came back to the States. I eventually met my wife and raised a family.

Now I am in a stage where I'm doing a lot of stuff I love and am very passionate about. My wife and I both are focusing on retiring. We love what we do; we both know we are making a difference;

we know we impact people. We can feel the ripple effect we have on people.

COLLEGE IS....

Amazing, but I don't believe we prepare young people in high school for what college is like. I also don't believe college is a setting for everyone. College is an experiment meant for people to succeed and some people do not succeed due to their lack of preparedness.

College is one step in the process of evolution from adolescent years to adulthood. I think it's part of that continuum some of us have to go through. For some, college influences and amazingly impacts us. College was not so pleasant for some of us, but it's part of this continuum that we go through. What I refused to buy into, though, is the concept that going to college and earning a degree is the only way to be successful. I don't think it's the only way to be successful. I don't think it should define you, should you choose not to attend college.

MY PHILOSOPHY

Don't change who you are because of your circumstance. Value people who are important to you. Sometimes we are busy so-called chasing this dream or who we think we should be, and we stop caring about people in our lives who we should hold dear.

Camila

Fisk University, BS Computer Science
Howard University, MS Computer Science
George Washington University –Strategic Project Manager Certificate/Certified Public Manager
Hometown: Wichita, Kansas
Age Group: 40s

Life Motto: *"If you learn, teach; if you get, give. I lived by that all my life."*

LIFE BEFORE COLLEGE

I believe my upbringing in a close-knit family positively shaped who I am. Today as an adult, I feel multi-generational households are best for raising children. You get to know different parts of yourself; at least I did...as far as loving yourself and loving Black people. I'm a charitable person; I volunteer everywhere. My upbringing has impacted my life.

When I was a young girl, I dreamt of becoming a news reporter. My mother drew me into journalism in high school by bringing me to journalism camps run by a national African American journalist. Attending the camp gave me the *Okay, you do well, you go to school* vibe. But when it was time to attend a university, my father shared with me coming in late from hanging out with my older cousins that I needed to attend FISC, and FISC did not have a journalism school. He didn't want journalism for me. Then my mother suggested I learn computer science because that's where the money is at, and that was it.

COLLEGE OR NAH?

My grandpa told me to go to college, so I did. Originally, I thought of college as being a place that babysits you until you become an adult. I thought it was all about hanging out. My initial thought was, who was going to take care of me? Eventually, I realized college was a new chapter in my life.

THE GREY AREA

My grey area is being a parent. Now that I have children, whatever I have a projection for has been put on hold or deferred until I can get my life together with forming a family.

My grey area is trying to connect pieces of what's supposed to happen in life and what is actually happening. Trying to figure out what I'm supposed to do, how to establish a plan, feed the kids, do homework, and figure out the pieces of what I want to do. It is grey because sometimes there isn't a bridge that I can see.

I believe the grey area is temporary. Eventually, something is going to click. Like okay, I'm making a connection, my brain is making that connection, and my body is making that connection. I'm going to act on it. If you act on it, it can't be grey. When all of those things meet, it can't be grey.

HAPPENSTANCE? FATE? OR BOTH?

I believe the ancestors have something for me, and sometimes I see these signs. I don't know if that's happenstance. I know the ancestors have something for me because I'm still evolving into this being. I'm still serving the community, whether by being a public servant or serving somebody in a way that assists others. So I don't know if that's karma… because someone helped me, I should help them.

#GOALS

My plan for my first year was to have as much fun as possible. I was a Wu-Tang fan, and I wound up finding girls of the same feather as me. So freshman year, I had the best time. In sophomore year, I planned to focus on computer science because the curriculum increased, and the program became more rigorous. I wanted to concentrate, but I also wanted to explore socially, university-wise. So I found kindred spirits in learning about African culture and learning more about the African diaspora.

My social plan in college was also to explore. Another part of my plan was to travel abroad. I traveled all over the place, trying to make that connection to the people who I met that were from all over the world during my sophomore year. I wanted to experience where they lived.

Post-graduation, an internship during my sophomore year, dictated what I was going to do. So post-graduation, I would not get a job; I would get my graduate degree and follow my grandmother's advice of being a scholar; I was like, this is what scholars do; they get their graduate degrees, then many more.

POST COLLEGE

After I graduated, I thought, *I've got to pay back these loans!* I knew I had been admitted to Howard with a full ride. So my first thought was *I better hurry and get to Howard*. Once I reached the university, I felt inadequate.

I was supposed to go straight to the PhD program from my master's program, but I switched to get a job. So I got a job on Howard's campus implementing PeopleSoft, and that's how it started.

These days I'm a wife and mom of two amazing girls. I am actively grooming them as far as learning about yourself, loving that you are Black; I have to do this every day.

I enrolled myself in the CPM program. I received two certificates. Now the work is paying off, but I need to push myself more. I've set deadlines for myself, so I can grow. To make it official, I'm adding it to my performance review. So now it's public for everybody to see.

COLLEGE IS...

An important tool to understand how the world works. I didn't take university studies, as I wish I would have. If I had done more, it would have impacted my decision about where I am in my career. I would have more concentration and pushed myself to be involved in different networking events. Those events in undergrad are typically a trajectory for more success.

College is an academic environment that is supposed to groom you, prepare you for being an adult and a professional in your field of choice. It's supposed to be a safe environment where mistakes can be made and where you can learn how to bounce back from them.

MY PHILOSOPHY

Do your homework. Treat college as a job, be selfish. I remember not being selfish. I was involved in activities where I should not have given up my time for the nonsense that could have impacted my life. Not being selfish with my time affected my academics. So be selfish with your time and your body, make a plan, and stick with it. Organize yourself; if you don't have organizational skills, you will not survive. You need to know yourself and know what your values are. If you don't value time and intelligence, then I don't think you will go far.

Hallo

CENTRAL TEXAS COLLEGE '08, ASSOCIATES
IN INTERDISCIPLINARY STUDIES

HOMETOWN: KILLEEN, TX

AGE GROUP: 30s

Life Motto: "*We are the creator of our worlds.*"

LIFE BEFORE COLLEGE

As a kid, I had those parents who would always tell me, "Do nothing half-assed." They were definitely behind me every step of the way, pushing and supporting me. As far as housework and schoolwork were concerned, there was a standard to meet. If I didn't do it right the first time, my parents would have me do it again until I got it right. They ingrained in me how to be mindful of my work.

I was a kid with a big imagination and bigger dreams. By the time I was in elementary school, I had decided to be a singer/songwriter. But, as I experienced later, there's a lot you go through in life to follow that path.

TALK GREY TO ME

There are so many sides to being a recording artist because you have to think about the music, the image, the networking, the politics, and even the criticism. I was running into many people with negative opinions on that career choice: *That's not a real job, that's not something you can succeed at, go to school instead.*

I also ran into people who are part of the business, some of whom lorded their position and power over people, making it painfully obvious the music 'business' is much more about the business and politics than the art. I was frustrated with trying to fit into that industry, and even more, overwhelmed by the creative process. You have to heavily depend on other people's creative and technical contributions unless you're producing, engineering, writing, and doing a hundred other things all on your own.

Eventually, I picked up a camera and started taking shots of myself with a timer/tripod setup. The idea was to use the photos as part of a press kit to accompany the music I worked on. I posted some photos on social media and got a lot of good feedback about them. People even inquired about rates. That's when I first realized there might be something in photography for me.

Picking up the camera was something I could do with no strings attached. I could be creative at that moment, and no one could stand in my way or create an obstacle for that. There was immediate gratification in being able to express myself freely and creatively. That satisfaction, coupled with the work ethic my parents taught me, led to me spending countless hours learning DSLR photography through reading, watching tutorials, and practice. Low and behold, it's what I'm doing for a living now.

COLLEGE OR NAH?

I attended college because I didn't have to pay for it at the time. If I had to pay for it, I probably wouldn't have gone. I was accepted at a few universities my senior year of high school; I almost went to Howard. When I was looking at tuition and fees, I thought *this was not happening*.

Even at a young age, I understood I didn't want to be in debt. The fear of being in debt kept me from going to Howard. I wasn't prepared or knowledgeable about scholarships or grants. My parents hadn't gone to college, so they didn't have that knowledge to pass on to me. Surprisingly, teachers and faculty at the school didn't teach us about attaining grants or scholarships either.

My dad was military, so I ended up going to a community college through the G.I. Bill. Continuing education after high school wasn't mandatory in my family. My dad took a few classes at the same community college I was enrolled at, but that was it. Growing up, I didn't see or hear of people going off for higher education. People either got a job, went to the military, got married, learned a trade, or were in jail. College didn't top the list of examples I saw for life after high school.

When I started college, it felt odd. I took a break between high school and college, so going back to school after living in the 'real world' felt a little like being a kid again in some ways. It was a little weird in that sense, but it was exciting too.

THE GREY AREA

Uncertainty is my definition of the grey area. Life is a journey where we're usually looking for fulfillment and purpose, and thinking about there being a finish line can leave many people feeling lost or confused about how to get there.

I wouldn't say I'm in the grey area currently. I feel I'm in a free-flowing area of goodness. Once you give into the universe and you don't focus on your ego, you find happiness in existence.

I don't know what's coming two years from now, but I know that I'm lucky right now. Opportunities continue to present themselves, and I can see them because I'm not struggling to find something else that my ego thinks it needs in the future.

HAPPENSTANCE? FATE? OR BOTH?

Both for sure. I believe in fate to an extent, not as the end-all, be-all. We have the responsibility and ability to influence our trajectory and shape our world.

I think the grey area might be synonymous with life. We don't know everything. There's nobody that knows everything, and I find that to be freeing. When you think about it, if there was no grey area then that would mean everything is controlled and set in stone. Where's the excitement in that? Where's the room for growth? Where's the room for something new?

When you think about God, you think about people. God is the Creator. People are creators. We're made in His image, and I feel like the grey area is the potential for creativity and possibilities. It's the potential for everything we are. Whether that's good or bad depends totally on choices and perspective.

#GOALS

My two-year plan while in college was to get in and get this over with. I was in the grey area. I was thinking, *What am I going to do?* I have to figure out what my major is going to be. So I was thinking about journalism, taking music classes or art classes. I was thinking about all these different ways to go. But, then I sat and thought because I was getting my associate's, I realized the classes I took would not exactly lead to whatever major I want to take after getting my associate's. I was taking general education classes. So I chilled out, took a breath, and said, "Let me get these two years out of the way."

POST COLLEGE

The first week after I got my degree, I was happy and relieved. But I was also thinking about what on earth I would use my associate's for. Although I didn't create a post-graduate timeline, I enjoy life and doing something I'm excited about.

COLLEGE IS...

What you make of it. Make sure you are educated *before* you get there.

MY PHILOSOPHY

As long as you learn to relax, you'll figure life out. Have an excellent support group of friends and family.

Charles

GRADUATED COLLEGE

AGE GROUP: 70s

Life Motto: *"I can do anything that I want to do; it may take me longer, but I can do anything or be anything that I want to be."*

LIFE BEFORE COLLEGE

Growing up in McComb, Mississippi, made me want education. Nobody in my family went to high school or graduated from college. My mother probably finished the 5th grade, and my father possibly finished the 8th grade. One of my older brothers was the first to graduate from high school. As soon as he graduated from high school, he went off to Detroit, Michigan, and started working for General Motors. He instilled work values into my life. He showed me that if you work hard, you can earn a decent living.

My dream as a child was to play professional sports. But, unfortunately, I hadn't picked out which one. I was pretty good at football, basketball, and baseball, but I didn't know which one to pursue.

Because I was a little skinny kid, I tried gaining weight to join one of the teams. I was 6'2 with no meat on my bones. No matter how much I ate, I could not gain any weight. So basketball was out, baseball was out, and football was out.

When I started first grade in 1965, the Civil Rights Act passed. We had an elementary school in my backyard, but my niece and I were sent to a segregated school because of the pilot program we were a part of. Going to this all-White school forced me to be as smart as the white kids. We had good books and good education, and I ended up being a nerd by going to this school. I didn't realize it at the time, but I was more concerned with reading and learning than I was with sports.

This led to my current situation because of my academic performance and how good I was in school. When the recruiters came to the school, you would take the military entrance exam, and most of the black kids scored high enough to get into the Army or the Marines, but they didn't score high enough to get into the Air Force. I and some of the other nerds scored high enough to get into the Air Force. So some of us decided that we were going to join the Air Force.

It was very sad that we set such low standards for ourselves, and other people couldn't see that I'm trying to set an example.

COLLEGE OR NAH?

To be competitive in the military, we had areas we had to fulfill. First, we had to do what we called professional military education, which encompassed all of our military courses. Then we had to take college courses to be a complete person. To get promoted to that 1 percent, you can't just do your military education; you have to do civilian education as well. So I had to go to college, which I thought I never would. However, I had to take college classes to get to that point. I only needed an associate's degree, so I got an associate's degree. Then I got my bachelor's degree in life after the military.

#GOALS

My four-year college plan took sixteen years. I knew it was going to take a while because, in the military, we change locations. When we change locations, the schools change, and many credits are not accepted, and we have to repeat courses. So I knew I would lose credits because we don't stay anywhere for four years.

When I graduated, I had already started planning my retirement from the military. I received my associate's degree in 1997. Later in life, I went back to school, and I completed thirty-six semester hours in two years. I had a full-time job, and I was a single parent. So what I planned to do was to graduate in 1999, which I did. I started building a house in '99, and in 2000, I planned to retire from the Air Force at age 40. My goal was to make it to E-9 Chief Master Sergeant by the time I was 20 years in, at which time I would have been 37. I did both.

POST COLLEGE

My feelings and thoughts after I graduated were, *I am educated. I can command a great salary, I have years of experience and education to support my wanted salary.* Everything that I believe I would get, based on experience and education, has happened.

Presently, I'm working for the government, and I am at the end of my third career. I have been a business owner; I have worked in the private industry, and I have worked in the Air Force. What I decide to do depends on how I feel. I may go back to school, finish my master's and start a PhD program. I just haven't decided what I am going to do yet.

COLLEGE IS...

An entity to get me the credentials to support the experience I already had. I had the experience, but I could not get the job or the salary that college degrees warranted without the paperwork. I needed a college degree to get that job. No matter how much experience I had, I needed a college degree.

I think college is very important. I am very much satisfied with my degrees; they have worked for me during my career. I have been very successful. When I speak to people, I remind them to continually pursue advanced education.

MY PHILOSOPHY

The biggest lesson I learned is to continue to educate yourself, whether in life or in education. Continue to get better and always read. I read at least one book per month. I have been retired now from the Air Force for 18 years. I counted all the books that I've read since I retired, and I've read pretty close to 200. So to continue to learn, grow, and continue to read. It keeps the mind active.

Mary

HOMETOWN: WEST COVINA, CALIFORNIA
SEATTLE UNIVERSITY SCHOOL OF LAW '05, J.D.
WRIGHT STATE UNIVERSITY '88, B.S. BUSINESS MARKETING
AGE GROUP: 50s

Life Motto: *"Please forgive me; I know not what I do. Ah, you seek to outlive me, but I want you to."*

LIFE BEFORE COLLEGE

Growing up, I learned that hard work, a loving heart, caring about yourself and your neighbors, and faith in God are the most important things. I wanted to be a lawyer and maybe someday get into politics. However, I experienced a dark time, so I became involved with creative writers. I became torn between being a lawyer and being into politics and helping my creative friends get their music published.

Instead of being a lawyer, I'm a paralegal, but I go to law school at night. So I'll probably be a pro bono lawyer and maybe have some public defense work when I finally pass the bar exam. However, being a paralegal has given me a lot of experience.

COLLEGE OR NAH?

I decided to go to college so I could get a law degree and be a lawyer. While college wasn't mandatory in my family, I was still expected to work hard. I had a clear understanding that nothing would be handed to me.

My parents valued a good education. They both have bachelor's degrees. Even though they were immigrants, they went to college, worked hard, and got a formal academic degree. If we did not go into business for ourselves, then we needed to continue to be educated.

When beginning college, I was sensitive and defensive because the girls were much worldlier than me. In addition, I was socially underdeveloped, so I felt defensive. To compensate for that, I made up for lost time and became a little promiscuous for about a year.

THE GREY AREA

A grey area is when black and white co-exist as one in equal portions. I learned from the Institute of Divine Metaphysical Research that Scripture and scientific evidence support the following: Things of the physical world are copying their superior, which is the invisible world, which Plato used to call the world of the form, the world of the pattern. When you look at physical reality and try to understand the historical underpinning in its interwoven physical impotence that navigates, it's when you look to physical realities and define an appropriate overlay. Of that physical structure of law and that hypothesis, you apply it to the physical reality you are attempting to discern and navigate.

Black and white are when the good guy and the bad guy are functioning as one, and they are equal to each other, and that's grey. I would say I'm in the black and white area because I am getting ready to retire. I believe the black area and the white area are always eternal, but our awareness of them even flows as the universe demands prior so.

HAPPENSTANCE? FATE? OR BOTH?

I believe God has laid out our lives and that we have agreed with God before we came down here that we will live this particular life to learn these particular lessons.

#GOALS

My original four-year plan took me five years because I got married. Then I got a divorce, and I finished my bachelor's degree shortly before I got divorced. My four-year plan was to get an undergrad degree and then go to law school.

POST COLLEGE

Post-graduation feelings and thoughts—well, let's get up and go to work on Monday for somebody! Whether it's a minimum wage job working for somebody, looking for something better, or it's a job that will allow me to study law.

I decided to join the military as a paralegal. I had some money that went toward my continuing education. I applied for the G.I. Bill went to law school at night, and I graduated.

I never quit my military day job, and now I'm retiring from the military.

To help me transition and help me take care of my family obligations, I am looking for weekend work, and then before I go right back into looking for work, I will take the bar exam. Then, I'll have a month or two where I don't have to work all the time, just part-time, and I'm going to study for the bar.

COLLEGE IS....

Necessary. Learning shows us facts and facets of the visible world and the invisible world that controls it. The physical is the puppet; the invisible world is the puppet master. Higher education, higher learning gives you insight into both worlds, not just the physical world.

MY PHILOSOPHY

Work hard, have faith, try to love people unconditionally as the Bible instructs us to. Then, if people harm you, try to forgive them so that you can be forgiven.

Julian

University of Maryland '16, College Park, B.S. Mechanical Engineering

Hometown: Gaithersburg, Maryland

Age Group: 20s

Life Motto: *"Fall in love with not your dream of success but your journey"*

LIFE BEFORE COLLEGE

Growing up, my parents instilled in me the understanding that I don't have the opportunity to be mediocre. I have to be great at anything I do. In one sense, they were very strict in their expectations, but in another sense, my parents gave me a lot of opportunities to explore my creative side. When I was young, my parents would put me in any activity they could get me in until one stuck. I started with sports. Soccer didn't go so well; basketball didn't go well. They put a clarinet in my hand, and I was pretty okay at that. I started blossoming when I started with trumpet and guitar. They were very supportive of my music playing, so it's a dualistic kind. They have high expectations for academic success and understand the value of exploring the creative side.

Oddly enough, I didn't have a vision for myself in the future until I was living it. I got asked that a lot when I was growing up, what I wanted to be, but I could not see myself as an older person. I know that's very weird to hear.

When I was in elementary school, I got into a fair amount of trouble because my attention was not to my teacher's standard. As a result, I was easily distracted, so my parents tested me for the gifted and talented program because they thought I was bored. From there, I got put on a separate track from most of my peers.

I went to a gifted and talented school for most of my 4th and 5th grade, and then the local math and science program for 6th-12th grade. What that meant was I was on a specialty course in a specialty program in a public school. So I was essentially surrounded by kids my age, but my classes were accelerated. Being placed in a competitive program forced me to become more competitive myself, which meant that I more or less had to study more, work more. Because I was in specialty programs, the major options surrounding college were doctor, computer science, mathematician, scientist, etc. So for me, engineering became the best choice.

COLLEGE OR NAH?

The decision to go to college was made for me, but I wasn't purely against it. Attending college was the next natural step, given who I was surrounded by. The first step on campus felt freeing. I was finally out on my own and could do whatever I wanted to do.

THE GREY AREA

As I experienced it, the grey area was stepping out of college, having gone through essentially all the steps I was meant to go through in my academic career and feeling pretty wholly unfulfilled. There was a whole path laid out for me. Especially because I had little time for self-discovery given the field I studied. I spent most of my life working towards a goal. And it was incredibly stressful because I subconsciously knew engineering wasn't all I was supposed to do. That led to some pretty tough mental time because everything until that point had an expiration date. You are in elementary school; it will end in 5th grade—middle school, end in 8th grade, high school, etc. But once you step out into the world, there is no expiration date; you are in it. It's very overwhelming to realize the next steps are purely your own, especially when you've been in a very structured academic environment. So I would say the grey area for me would be when the path that was made for your ends, and you have to define the rest of it.

I believe the grey area will last a varying amount of time-based on what you do while in the grey area. Although you may have a lot of stuff going on in your life at that moment, you need to take time to define your next step. If you don't, your grey area may stay with you.

HAPPENSTANCE? FATE? OR BOTH?

I believe in both. Specifically for me, on top of engineering, I discovered I was meant to be a musician. Everyone has their purpose within the tribe, and I imagine our brains know what that is, whether our brains are to be a creative mind, a supportive mind to be a leader, etc. So if our lives are not reflective of what we're meant to do, I believe it leads to many mental issues and instability because you are taking someone who was meant to do one thing and forcing them to do another. Maybe that person doesn't know what they are meant to do, but I'm sure there's some kind of dopamine receptors that aren't being fired off or whatnot, that will show your brain, *Okay this might be fine, but this isn't what this person was meant to do.* Our generation feels that more than most because we have the opportunity to get so many quick dopamine fixes that it becomes so obvious when there is a big part of it we're missing. I like to avoid the term fate. I don't think our destiny comes from a higher power. I think it's kind of an almost biological fate. Let's say you are meant to be a carpenter, and you never knew that you were meant to be a carpenter. Or you were put on a track that took you nowhere near carpentry. Then, years down the road, you may be an excellent electrician, but you may not be as happy or fulfilled as you would be if you were a carpenter.

#GOALS

I had the typical four-year engineering program as my plan. After that, my vision was pretty much to just get the job after college, which was as far as the plan went.

POST COLLEGE

I had pretty much mental crisis after mental crisis, to be honest. Post-graduation, I felt I was running a marathon and reaching the end and winning, but then all the lights turned out, and there was no one in the stands.

What I learned from college was different from what I thought I was going to learn from college. Walking into college, I thought I would learn such an extensive understanding of engineering that I would be an encyclopedia. Instead, I figured out by the end that the key takeaway from college was learning how to learn and how to deal with people. And in that way, I felt I was greatly prepared for the world when I graduated, just not prepared in the way I had expected.

I didn't have a post-college timeline because I couldn't even envision it. But what has changed is the previous imagination that I would get the job, and then that was going to be it. I kind of reached a point in my professional career where I feel I could take a break and make a little music. It's not so rigid anymore. I have a kind of new respect for taking time to discover what I want to do, and I've realized life isn't as rigid as it may seem.

Right now, I am working as a control engineer for a control engineering contracting firm. So what that means is I do programming for automated systems with a good amount of travel in there. It's very rewarding. On top of that, I play for 2-3 bands from time to time. So I'm kind of semi-professionally playing gigs, making money, and doing other passionate projects. Just living the musician's dream.

COLLEGE IS...

What you make of it. College can be a four-year summer camp, or it can be a four-year boot camp, depending on many factors. You can get a lot or very little out of college. Your expectation management and I guess viewing it with a critical eye is very important.

When I was applying to college, it seemed an obvious choice for everyone. However, having graduated, my biggest revelation is that college is most certainly *not* for everyone. I was fortunate that I went into a field where I can comfortably pay off my loans. But I know my experience isn't typical. I got a lot out of college, and what I studied very greatly aligned with how my brain works. So it wasn't very difficult for me at the time. When I graduated, I was able to get a lot of value from my degree. However, through personal connections, I've seen how if you pick something you were passionate about and it doesn't pay well, you are in a worse financial position than if you were to just find another way to acquire those skills. Or even worse, if you pick something that pays well, but you weren't good at it, then you may graduate with a piece of paper and without those skills and still be in a poor financial situation. So given the rising cost of education and the fact that more and more people are getting educated, I firmly believe college is not always the best option for everybody.

MY PHILOSOPHY

Don't be afraid to sacrifice for your future. I had to make sacrifices most of my life, so making sacrifices in college wasn't a big jump for me. Delaying gratification in your early years will set you up for a lot more success later on. By that same token, don't be afraid to explore new things and learn more about yourself. If you stick to that path, you may find when you emerge, there is nothing in front of you, and you don't know enough about yourself to make that next move. They are not mutually balanced here cause I'm pretty sure I just said two conflicting things. But understand the importance of finding your reason to be your calling. It may not be exactly what your career is, but take the time, take the energy to at least explore, and try to find what that is if you don't know already.

Lauren

ATTENDED SINCLAIR COMMUNITY COLLEGE AND
STUDIED INDUSTRIAL ENGINEERING

HOMETOWN: DAYTON, OH

AGE GROUP: 40s

Life Motto: *"Be the person who holds the pen to your own destiny. Don't let another person hold your pen when you write your memoir of life. No one."*

LIFE BEFORE COLLEGE

I was raised in a household of a single mother. My mother had support from her mother and her father, but there was a lot of negativity in our home. People belittled us because we were my father's children. To them, we couldn't do anything well—negative conversation against us from being just children. My mother did not squash it; she rolled with it because she had bitterness toward him, not realizing how it affected us. It came to a point where it didn't affect us anymore because we no longer cared about their opinion of us or anything they thought. They ceased to matter. That strengthened us in a way. If other people get stupid, we come to a point where we agree to disagree, and then we are done. That type of thinking gives birth to independent thinking. My siblings and I were born in poverty, and we wanted better, so we started working at an early age to get what we desired. We didn't get into the criminal route; we wanted to get material possessions the right way through hard work. Learning work ethics, building skills, realizing you also need more education to get more money. We started identifying with the things to help propel us to success.

During my adolescence, I wanted to be a teacher. I evolved to be a teacher of youth. I realized being an educator in today's society does not pay well, and the role of taking on children during the greater percentage of their waking hours was similar to being a surrogate parent, parental educator, and I didn't want that.

Students are being molded by their teachers; above anyone else, they are being molded by their environment being in the school setting. If the school setting is geared toward success, the higher the percentage of the children will be geared toward success. Suppose a school setting is geared toward sex, drugs, destructive and counterproductive behavior. In that case, you will have a large portion of those children taking on those behaviors and not being constructive into becoming an adult. This has been taking place 8 hours, 5 days a week, for 12 years. That is a large portion of molding. Students are being molded by their school environment more than by anything else.

COLLEGE OR NAH?

When beginning college, I was already a mother, and I wanted better for my children. My mother didn't teach us anything about college. She just told us to go to school. I didn't have a true concept about college because, at the time, there wasn't a role model to inspire us about why we should go to college or even take me to a college.

A conversation I had with an African girl reminded me of why it's important to tell Black kids about college. We talked about life experiences, and I told her if I could do life differently, I would focus on learning statistics on your race, your gender, and your age group. Statistics that go against your race, the complication of your race, gender, and age group. You have a lot of Black people who are single mothers. You have a lot of them who have been exposed to drugs and premarital sex. You have people taking downfalls that keep them from their purpose. When you encounter those people, you make sure you encounter some people who try to get you to be a percentage of those statistics.

THE GREY AREA

The grey area is living by who you were made to be versus who you truly are. We are limited from the time we are born; we are told what age we are, how many months we are, even in the womb, we are told how many months pregnant our parents are. We've even been tagged by aging from the moment of conception. They are telling us about our age. I truly feel that we are reincarnated. We are ageless beings; science has proven it. And if anybody has gotten into meditation and become one with the spirit in them, they will tell you they've had past life connections. These unexplainable events can only happen to a person having a past life. So as long as someone lives their life by how they were made to be by their parents, by society, by external forces, they will always be in a grey area. Tribal family members learn before naming the child; they observe the child's nature, and by observing the child's nature, they communicate with the spirits, they give the child vision quests. They can properly name the child according to what has been shown before them. So that's one grey area.

The other grey area I feel is learning your soul. Often, people in this society want to please others, be part of a clique, be part of a group of some type, and assimilate. And by assimilating, we are living in a grey area because we are not true to ourselves. We are true to what is acceptable. *Everyone's doing this, so I should do that.* Well, you are living in that grey area. Because you are not living by your soul, what makes your soul happy, and what brings your soul harmony.

HAPPENSTANCE? FATE? OR BOTH?

I believe for every action, there is a reaction; there is an opposite or parallel. I believe in that because that is quite apparent in all things we encounter. I believe when you meditate, you see yourself being guided; you will experience guidance. Sometimes I've watched cop shows, and when you see them being apprehended, you see something that taught them to be like this. Something told them not to do that. Question that energy, question that source. The more you put your focus on that energy and that source, that it is going to be your absolute truth. I'm not a religious person because man has touched it, but I believe in that source. The source that you find you question it, you go to a relationship with it, that's your religion, that should be your absolute truth, that should not fail you at all.

POST COLLEGE

I wanted to focus on taking care of my family. I was happy to go to work and provide for my family. That's all that mattered to me.

COLLEGE IS…

Enslavement to the system. If you are studying at a community college, you might stand a better chance. However, if you are going to a university, you are pledging your life into debt. It should not be that way. Colleges should not offer any program if it does not offer a positive outlook for job growth. If the college doesn't offer positive job growth, then it is wasting people's time.

MY PHILOSOPHY

At the end of the day, find what makes you happy, what agrees with your soul, and then build upon it.

Those who have been made the victim of their upbringing, it's not you. It's those who let you down, those who corrupted your trust, exposed you to drugs, sex, activities that are not productive. Make peace with that in yourself; realize those people were sick people. Now you have a thing called adulthood, where you can make those choices and take control of them. You don't have to be a victim as an adult; make peace with your inner child. Trauma is a risk.

Don't rely on other people's words. Be focused on the action above all things. When it comes to love, love yourself first. Take respect over love any day. All chaotic experiences evolve from a lack of respect.

Sierra Leone, American Poet

University of Toledo, B.S. Criminal Justice
Wright State University '03, M.S. Applied Behavioral Science
Wright State University '19, M.B.A
Hometown: Toledo, Ohio
Current Residence: Dayton, Ohio

Life Motto: *"Let the beauty of what you love, be what you do." - Rumi;* *"I am new power; I trust my heart and the aliveness that flows from within." - Sierra Leone.*

LIFE BEFORE COLLEGE

I think having a mother who lived in Toledo, Ohio, and came from very humble roots and urban background, as well as having a father who grew up in the Deep South and was very well off, gave me an opportunity to experience life from a unique perspective. I had the opportunity to live a portion of my life with my mother and a portion of my life with my father. Those experiences shaped how I saw the world and how I've interacted with people. Those experiences allowed me to see who people really were.

As a child, my dream was to grow up and be a homicide detective. I thought, well, I encounter a lot of crime, I can go to school to be a homicide detective and take on the world. However, in my heart of hearts, I wanted to be an artist. I wrote poetry. Although, at the time, I didn't know it was poetry. It was just my journal. I wanted to be a poet, an artist. But I never knew a living soul or any family member who was an artist. I had only seen artists on TV.

I never thought college was something realistic for a person coming from my experience. College wasn't mandatory in my family, but since I was in Upward Bound, it shaped my perspective about what to expect. I was in the Upward Bound program from 8th grade until my freshman year of college. During that time, going to college was a way out; and it was what was being done on *The Cosby Show* and *A Different World*. But once I started, college truly became a refuge that I never wanted to leave.

COLLEGE LIFE

In college, life happened to me. I was quite active. I was a student leader and the president of the Women's Organization for the Advancement of African American Women. I ended up being Vice President of the Black Student Union, as well as leading all sorts of classes. I was the president of the largest community service club on campus. I had the opportunity to live an amazing life in college and to be supported by wonderful people.

Studying corrections in college was my first step toward becoming a homicide detective. I was in school and committed to my initial professional goal. Before the end of my second year, one of the professors pulled me to the side and said, "You need to leave the major or at least go on to get your full criminal justice degree. You can't stop at the two-year mark and take a job in the field." I asked, "Why?" He told me, "This isn't the life for you. You are so much greater than this." He told me that this job ends in divorce. One of his sons committed suicide, and he had several addictions himself. He could not imagine allowing me to stay on that path without sharing his lived truth.

I did complete the corrections associate's degree. Then I went on to complete my bachelor's in criminal justice. I was the first person in my family to graduate from college with a college degree. My grandmother had 22 kids. I had 44 first cousins. It was a very emotional day.

CAREER CHOICES

I worked for a juvenile treatment facility. While working there, my mentality shifted from corrections to treatment. I now know that people can be healed, and can change, versus this hardnosed hard-core prison correction system where I'm just here to lock you up, treat you like cattle, and do my job.

So, working in treatment, initially while in college, influenced my mind state. I was hired to be a forensic counselor inside of the Lucas County jail, and I loved it, but it was a lot on me. It was heavy. The two years I worked there, I never wrote. Amidst the negative energy at the jail, I felt smothered.

THE GREY AREA

The grey area is simply the inability to remove limitations. Today, I'm very clear about my life's purpose and the direction my life is going towards. I'm very clear the universe can only conspire to give us exactly what we expect, not what we want. So, if I'm expecting to keep living in this space where I didn't have a rooted connection to things because my parents didn't, and the generation before them did not, then I'm going to continue to be faced with those experiences. However, if I could wrap my mind around the idea that I'm simply experiencing the ceiling of my limitations, then I can see past them, and I can see past the grey area.

I believe the grey area is a permanent space because it's a state of mind. It's like being in DC or any other city. When you leave, DC is still going to exist; DC is not going to go anywhere just because you are not there. It will exist. So, the grey area is a permanent place, it's not a permanent place where you have to take up residence. There's always going to be people in that grey area, in these spaces and that state of mind, because I feel the grey area is a state of mind. It's a choice. So, if you choose to live beyond the grey area, you will not be there, but someone else will.

In the grey area, what we're up against is what some would call a terror barrier or underminer. When I'm in a grey space or working through those dark spaces, it's just fear of the unknown. Then it's me recognizing that this barrier is up, this limitation, this underminer showed up and made me feel like I don't know what I'm doing, I don't know where I'm going. I can't achieve what it is I want to achieve at this very moment. This is me recognizing that it's there for me to understand; F.E.A.R. is "false evidence appearing real." Moreover, the grey area is false evidence appearing real. Fear is not real, but the journey is. I need to pray; I need to look fear right in its face and move past that limitation.

HAPPENSTANCE? FATE? OR BOTH?

"I plan, God plans, and God is the best planner." What has happened for me in my life is that I would say to God, or say to myself or the universe, what I want or desire. I might say I want to take a specific route. If I surrender the how and stop trying to figure out how it will happen and allow that space to be held gently by the universe and by God and the infinite mind, then it can manifest much quicker. Because the route that I planned to take and doing it my way might take me ten years to get there, versus me surrendering to the path that's unfamiliar or unknown that I didn't plan for and getting there tomorrow.

MY CURRENT JOURNEY

What I have found is that there is no one path to your being. I have taken many detours along my journey. Yet, I have found that poetry has been a constant. While life was happening, I always made room for my voice and poetry while serving the greater community. My poetry has been permanently hung in the Dayton, local library; My husband Nate and I recently won a governor's award for the work we do in world creative arts. We just wrapped on a decade of producing live theater for urban creative arts. I still have the same drive, the same will to do the work. I already have a master's in the study of human behavior, and I've just completed my MBA. Nate and I are in the process of producing a live stage play with the University of Dayton. I also graduated from spiritual school in the summer of 2019. These are exciting times!

Now, I travel, and I'm a commissioned poet and full-time entrepreneur. I've worked in healing education, and art and those are the things that I do. I have clients, I consult with school districts, and I bring art to the stage, across the state of Ohio.

COLLEGE IS...

A place where you discover who you are or begin to embark on the path to knowing who you are. College is a beginning and an end.

MY PHILOSOPHY

Being you is enough. You are enough. That's all; you are enough.

Alison

ATTENDED LONG ISLAND UNIVERSITY AND STUDIED MUSIC
HOMETOWN: DAYTON, OH
AGE GROUP: 20s

Life Motto: "*Everything is temporary. Everything is perfect. Everything has its balance.*"

LIFE BEFORE COLLEGE

I traveled a lot when I was a child, so I learned nothing lasts forever. And since nothing lasts forever, there's no need to hold on to anything you can always outgrow. Whenever I feel I'm in a temporary situation, people wanting to leave my life or whatever, I don't fight. They were in my life for a particular time frame to teach me something, and I was their life for a particular time frame to teach them something.

As a child, I had several dreams. The major dream I'm going for right now is becoming a singer/songwriter. I can see growth in it, so that's the reason I'm so ecstatic about it. I also thought about being a teacher. However, I felt being a teacher wasn't for me because I feel teachers are underpaid. Since they are underpaid in American society, I would rather take on that stress as a parent rather than a professional.

In life, I learned to follow the flow of the river. If you follow the flow instead of fighting the current, it will not be hard. When you fight against the current, you have lessons you have to learn. As well as have different things you're going to go through; you will experience turmoil. I learned to not fight against the grain. Don't fight what's presented to you; either learn from it or receive the blessing from it.

COLLEGE OR NAH?

I didn't want to go to college, actually. But I attended college, and I wish I'd taken a two-year break before I went.

When I was a child, I didn't think I would go to college because I thought I was dumb. I was always told I was dumb or stupid by adults that I knew. But I knew I wasn't dumb; I was very self-aware. I didn't believe I wasn't dumb until I moved to New York. New York basically raised me as the woman I am today, which is why I say I'm from New York.

THE GREY AREA

A grey area is an age group, anywhere from 17-23. Everyone's going to experience that one grey area where you are excited about it. Once you are in there, you learn about having credit, renter's insurance, rental history, car insurance. You also learn about experiencing bonds with people; not everyone is going to be on the same page as you. Find your own agenda; it makes no sense to build a man up for eleven years, and he ends up leaving you for a white woman.

I experienced my grey area at 21, like a seed turning into a flower. I understood the meaning of life at 21; everything has a purpose or a reason.

The grey area lasts as long as you want it to. The grey area is temporary, but some people never grow out of the grey area because they do not allow themselves to grow and flourish in life.

HAPPENSTANCE? FATE? OR BOTH?

Both. Sometimes we can create our own curses and our own blessings. We can block our own curse and block our own blessing at the same time, too. Certain things are definitely given to us and provided for us. But we also create our own path. It's like saying the universe blessed you with a pen, a journal, and some snacks to help you generate thought. Life is yours to scribe.

#GOALS

My goal for college was to start and finish in four years, then I was going to make my music career. Be rich and famous by 25, have a poppin' credit score. I was going to do a lot of traveling and meet people in the music industry.

POST COLLEGE

College is for mature people; kids shouldn't go to college when they hit 17. You should be at least 21 to go. I say that because you need to allow yourself to live in your grey area and mature in it. When you go to college at 21-25, take it seriously. Not everyone needs to go to college. You don't have to go to college for you to function in this world. I had to stop going to school, work, then go back to school, etc. Now I know I don't need college to do what I want to do. I don't look at college as that important. I still want a degree, but right now, I have other things I want to focus on, like working on my first EP and mixtape.

COLLEGE IS...

A place for growth—I low-key feel college is a scam. Well, I don't know; I can't say it's a scam. Depends on the person and what you are trying to do. If you are going in undecided, then don't go. If your major is liberal arts, don't go.

MY PHILOSOPHY

If you go into college with the mindset of the party, then college is not for you. On the other hand, if you go there with a plan and know what you want, then go. Don't let friends and family pressure you into going to a place you're not sure you want to go to. That's your time you are spending trying to make people happy while you are not happy.

Willie

SOUTHERN NEW HAMPSHIRE UNIVERSITY
'19, B.A. CRIMINAL JUSTICE
HOMETOWN: PHILADELPHIA, PA
AGE GROUP: 20s

Life Motto: *"To keep your life exciting, always make your bucket list."*

LIFE BEFORE COLLEGE

My upbringing gave me the perspective of glass half-full rather than half-empty. When I was growing up as a kid, I had things, but not the new things everybody else had. My mom could afford things, just not designer. Because she had two kids, she focused on getting us the necessities and not name-brand items. I was teased a lot in school until I busted back, and the kids would say that I was funny. I realized kids can be obliviously ignorant or mean and wouldn't know that they're mean and think it's just all fun and games. I had to be my own self-esteem booster. At home, my sisters picked on me because I was the only boy. At school, kids would say to me, "You ain't got on Polo; your sneakers are still old."

But at the end of the day, I didn't care if they talked about me; if my mom is good, I'm good. But it took a while for me to get there and have that self-reflection because it didn't come until 9th grade, to be honest.

During my adolescence, I dreamt of becoming a writer. Even as a child, I was in the 2nd grade writing stories. I always wanted to write because I can create the entire universe when I write, and I control what's on paper. For those reasons I love to write.

COLLEGE OR NAH?

I decided to go to college to better myself. In high school, I never thought about college. I love to read and write; I just wasn't into the complete education thing. I was never big on education. Finally, in high school, I sat down and spoke to my mentor, and she said I wouldn't be able to do many things without a degree because society wants me to have a degree.

I knew cousins who graduated from college. We talked about college, but college wasn't essential. I don't believe many of my aunts or uncles or mom or father have a college degree. In my immediate family, my little sister is the only one who got her degree.

THE GREY AREA

I don't believe in coincidences at all. I realize not everything is up to fate, but certain things in life are going to happen regardless of the choices you make during life. I also feel many of the choices you make help shape the path you are on. So my ideology of life is that I create my destiny, but certain milestones and checkpoints will be inevitable. Those checkpoints and milestones can be good or bad.

The grey area is your mindset. Because you can have the mindset of being complacent and don't know who you are. You see the grey area and think you can push yourself forward, but you don't. Ultimately you are in the grey area. However, if you have a mindset of, *I have to do better*, then I feel the grey area is a small portion of your life.

#GOALS

Initially, when beginning college, my four-year plan was to get in, get out, and start teaching. However, my plan wound up being a six-year plan. I have sustained myself as an adult, now I'm back in college. My plan is to get the degree, move up the fire academy ranks, and start a real estate business. I also want to retire from the fire academy as early as possible. Then do real estate for 5-6 years, making sure I make really good investments. Last, I plan to open up a bookstore and live the rest of my life with my wife and kids.

COLLEGE IS....

As an organization out to take people's money, I have to pay you to teach me? I view college as a tool for someone who wants to propel in the real world.

MY PHILOSOPHY

You can't always account for life. We plan many things for ourselves for life to throw us a crazy curveball. Your plans can come to fruition, but there are also unknown things that pop up out of the blue that you can't predict.

Marie

ATTENDING SINCLAIR COMMUNITY COLLEGE AND
STUDYING VISUAL COMMUNICATIONS
(FUTURE PLANS TO TRANSFER TO FULL SAIL
UNIVERSITY TO STUDY ANIMATION)
HOMETOWN: DAYTON, OH
AGE GROUP: 20S

Life Motto: *"Carpe diem. Seize the day. Never settle in life."*

LIFE BEFORE COLLEGE

I always knew I wanted to go to college and get a higher learning experience. My family encouraged me to pursue higher learning. During my last year in high school, I was very passionate about art. When I talked to my mom about my goals, she said, "You might want to do art, but you may need to look into another career." I love art, but I knew I needed a real job. So I was in and out of school while balancing my passion for art and figuring out what to pursue as a major that would be profitable.

My dream as a kid was to work at Pixar or Nickelodeon and eventually make my cartoons and see them be enjoyed by others and putting smiles on everybody's faces.

In high school, art was my favorite subject. I was in and out of school, so my majors were English, engineering, and law. I didn't finish college, but I was there for a few semesters trying to figure out if a degree in English, engineering, or law was what I wanted. I decided to pursue art as education because it is a subject that I am passionate about. I want to be happy and do something I love, rather than make a lot of money and be miserable.

COLLEGE OR NAH?

I knew I wanted to go to college. I wanted to do something art-related. When I was in high school, I was running track, and colleges were looking at me for scholarships, but things didn't work out that way. During that time I felt a bit lost. I felt I would not get into the program I wanted at the school I wanted. But I also knew I wanted to be there because I wanted to take my art further.

College wasn't obligatory for me, but it was suggested. I knew college was expensive. I didn't want to have loans. I feel loans are the deal of the devil because of the interest you have to pay. I felt college was one thing you just have to do if you want to get to a better place and not work at a crappy job. Then again, you don't necessarily need college to get to where you want to in life, except for a few required programs. I attended college because I wanted to have formal art training and cultivate my skills.

THE GREY AREA

I would say I was in the grey area when trying to figure out my career path. I was trying to figure out what career I wanted while overcoming my doubt.

The grey area is a designated area for finding yourself. In this area, you are finding yourself and aren't sure about what you want to do; you feel lost. Even though you know deep down inside what you want to do you are doubting you aren't trusting yourself to go for what you want. The doubt you experience is the grey area.

You can live in the grey area and always try to figure out your purpose in life while being in a dead-end job, or you can live in the grey area and hit that moment and make a change to your life path and do what's best for you.

#GOALS

After my first semester at a community college, I planned to go to Buffalo State University, run track, and study art. Then, post-graduation, move to Florida, California, or New York City and Work at Universal Studio, or work on doing something creative, like TV production or video production. But I had nothing planned much further than that.

POST COLLEGE

Now that I'm not in school, I'm frustrated because I felt I needed college to succeed. I felt like if I'm not in school, I'm going to be behind, like everybody else. I probably won't ever reach my career goals. I had a strict timeline. Go to school, graduate, and work.

Currently, I am enrolled in a community college studying business communication and working full-time. It's pretty hard; sometimes, I need time to finish projects I don't have time to do because of work. Sometimes, I have to get up early before work and work on projects. I had to tell my job that school comes before work. Hopefully, my employers do not fire me for that.

COLLEGE IS...

While I feel college helps you get to where you need to go if you want a better career. I sometimes feel college tries to get money from you, and I do not like that.

MY PHILOSOPHY

You may not find your career path right away, and it's okay. I recommend taking time out and getting to know yourself. If you are passionate about something creative, I recommend you follow your passion. The money will come, and if not, you can always find avenues to get your way out and get your money. There is always another way.

Leila

AGE GROUP: 50S

HOMETOWN: DAYTON, OH

ATTENDED UNIVERSITY OF CINCINNATI

Life Motto: *"Your setback is your setup for your comeback."*

LIFE BEFORE COLLEGE

My parents were pretty strict on me growing up and provided me with a solid education by getting me into specialty schools to help form the person I am today.

As a teen, I went to Patterson Co-op. I was going to school for two weeks, and I was going to work for two weeks. So I always knew I wanted to be some type of professional. I didn't know what type of professional job I wanted, but I was an accounting major in high school. Then with my co-op job, I worked for GM, and once they found out the skills I had, they sent me to study engineering.

I was blessed to have really good people in life to help with my career move. Because it was my step-grandmother when I was attending the University of Cincinnati who got me into working for the newspaper. From there my newspaper supervisor and management team put me in an advanced leadership role.

COLLEGE OR NAH?

I wanted to get out of my parents' house, so I went to college. My granddaddy was like, "You gotta get out of my house at 18." He said that even though we didn't live in the same house. I wouldn't say going to college was mandatory. My grandparents were happy whether I was studying a trade or going to college. They were happy as long as I was doing something productive.

While I was in highschool, I had many friends who attended college, so I had some insight into what to expect which helped me with the transition. But what they didn't tell me was how poor I was going to be. When you and your best friend are going through each other's change to get twenty-five cents for a candy bar, that's when you know you're poor. Like, figure it out.

THE GREY AREA

Well, I read this book; your setback is a setup for your comeback. It helped me after I lost my career after 20 years in the newspaper business. Because, as you are aware, newspapers are pretty much a dinosaur, and with the Internet, it undoes everything about a newspaper career. Once you get into the newspaper career, you die with that position, as far as within that industry. But with the coming of age of the Internet, everyone sits down and has a serious discussion. What do I want to be when

I grow up? What skills can you transfer into creating a new you? That's why the Lord just put it on my heart: Head on down to the Carolinas. Now I'm still in media communications, working for the cable company. So I could transfer that skill set into what I'm doing now.

In my opinion, the grey area is temporary. It's just a season. In anybody's lifetime, you'll have different seasons; it's just what type of season it is. Is it a season of upward mobility where you'll constantly be challenged?

Anyone who tells you that you will not go through ebbs and flows with your life is lying to you as far as your career. Honey, you're going to have that no matter what; it's all about how you react to it. Recognize where you are and don't allow it to defeat you. Look at it as a challenge; you'll overcome and develop a strategy on how you're going to get out of it.

#GOALS

My four-year plan was to graduate with my degree in accounting. But then, in my second year, I started working at the newspaper and saw how much money I could make. So I kind of got money hungry.

POST COLLEGE

Once I discontinued school, I was a happy little camper because I was making a lot of money. I would have finished college, but I didn't have the money to continue with my college. Now I know I can make money, and I don't need a degree.

COLLEGE IS....

Great! I think everyone should go to college. That's where you are going to learn how to deal with your independence, how to network, and meet friends. College is going to give you survival skills and is going to test you. There's a lot of stuff you can take from college and transition it into life.

MY PHILOSOPHY

Have a dream regardless of how lengthy or big it may be. You're going to succeed either way, whether or not you make it, because at least you are striving for some type of goal.

Calvin

Attended Bauber College and studied Fashion Merchandising

Hometown: Bronx, NY

Age Group: 20s

Life Motto: *"Make the money; don't let the money make you. Or my pop favorite one: A promise is a comfort to a fool. Don't let people be out here promising you nothing, like, "Oh yeah, so and so they're gonna get me this, so I'm just gonna wait and get it." If you can get it yourself, go get it yourself."*

LIFE BEFORE COLLEGE

When I was young, I had no idea what I wanted to do when I grew up. I had a thing for fashion, though. Fashion came naturally to me. My passions for clothes came because my mom was mad cheap with clothes. I had to teach myself how to dress. I would go to the store, buy all the plain shirts that didn't have logos on them, and begin putting clothes together. Then later in high school, my counselor suggested I become a stylist, so I peeped into that a little bit.

COLLEGE OR NAH?

Going to college wasn't mandatory in my family. It was just something I saw on TV. My high school brought in some colleges to talk to us. One college representative came and spoke about their fashion program, and I was interested. So I thought, *Let me give it a shot.*

THE GREY AREA

The grey area is a little bit of everything. Karma could play into it because if you are a mean person, you will get what you give, but sometimes things aren't meant to happen, so that's why they don't work out. You might try something, see it going wrong, and it's just because it wasn't meant to happen. The grey area is temporary. But if you give up, it's going to be permanent.

HAPPENSTANCE? FATE? OR BOTH?

I believe in fate. For example, you might wear the same sneakers every single day. You might have money to buy new ones, but you wear the same shoes. One day you walk outside, a nail runs in your shoe, and now you have to buy new shoes. You may think *I just happened to step on a nail.* In actuality, it was probably time to get rid of your shoes. That was just a sign. I think everything happens for a reason. You may think something just happened at that moment, but you will know why that particular moment happened later on in life.

POST COLLEGE

I discontinued school because it cost too much. Why do people have to pay so much to go to a school, which is similar to high school? What is different?

Even though I didn't finish college, I still style other people. In the meantime, I've gotten into graphic design. I didn't think I would go into that area because I am not familiar with graphic design, but I became good at Photoshop and Illustrator, so it's working out.

As of now, I'm an entrepreneur. We have a hookah company that makes everyday money. I'm also working on the clothing line, which does not blow up overnight; it takes time.

COLLEGE IS...

Like a fancy high school, but with more freedom. College is also a scam, you see that *scam likely* pop up on your phone. Unless you are taking a business class, college almost teaches you to work for people. If you want to win, you can't work for anybody. The doctors and lawyers that are out here in these fancy cars own their own firms. You don't want to be good at working for somebody; you want to work for yourself.

MY PHILOSOPHY

If you don't like something, don't invest all of your time into it and look for something else. If you do like something, invest your time in it. But if you don't see yourself moving forward, in whatever you are investing your time in, move on. Some things are just not meant to be. After a couple of years, you don't see yourself moving forward, pack it up and go.

Jada

ATTENDED AMERICAN UNIVERSITY AND STUDIED SOCIOLOGY

HOMETOWN: WASHINGTON, DC

AGE GROUP: 60s

Life Motto: *"It's corny but, do unto others as you would have them do unto you. Because again, if you do ugly stuff, eventually it's gonna come back to visit you."*

LIFE BEFORE COLLEGE

I'm a Baby Boomer. So growing up in the '50s and '60s was interesting because that was a tumultuous time. Growing up in DC, I was around different people, although I lived in Black neighborhoods and went to Black schools. I just had a regular life. My parents were somewhat strict. Well, my mom was strict. She enforced the importance of being a good person, having moral character, as a female, always being a lady and that kind of thing. Some of those things still resonate with me today.

I can remember wanting to be a nurse, which is interesting because math and science were *not* my friends. When I got closer to high school, I was in a dance company. I was interested in being a dancer, but I never shared it with anybody because dance wasn't something that you do. Most of my family migrated from the South and believed that you were supposed to get a good government job once you got out of school, and that was your life.

My path was a mess! After high school, I went to college, but I wasn't prepared for it. Although my parents encouraged me to go to college, they didn't talk about the process. So I flunked out my first year. Not necessarily because I couldn't do the work, but more so, I didn't have the right habits to discipline myself to do the work. So from there, it was like, "Okay, what now?" I went to computer school. I finished that, and I had a couple of jobs, but I wasn't happy. So, eventually I became a flight attendant. I did that for several years, and I loved it! But when my daughter came, I had to pursue a different career.

I never really felt like I would want a 9-5 job, so from there, I went into real estate for several years. But then, the market changed, and I have this child now, so I decided to work for corporate America.

While I was raising my child, all of my choices were driven by how it would affect her. So, therefore, I didn't pursue any ambition that would cause me to travel or work late or things like that because my complete focus was my child. As a single parent, I wanted to be involved in her life, so I put a lot of my personal ambitions aside.

COLLEGE OR NAH?

I went to college because I got a full scholarship. I actually hate to say that out loud because to blow a full scholarship is crazy. I had a full scholarship, room, board, and work-study at American University.

Since my family didn't pressure me to attend college, I didn't have a perspective about it when I was younger. I remember when I started college, I felt excited. Even though I grew up in the city, I met new people, and I felt fairly exposed. In hindsight, I was pretty naïve.

THE GREY AREA

Interestingly enough, my grey area is in my spiritual life. My mother raised me in the church. I do things my mother puts me in, and I participate in those things. Now, I'm an adult, and I have a child. I participate in the activities I have her in. Now that she's grown and has her own life, I feel I'm in a grey area. I'm like, okay, what am I supposed to be doing now? Who am I? What am I supposed to do in my spiritual world? I'm not going to be with the junior choir; I'm not going to be with the Girl Scouts. So where is my interest? That, for me, is a very grey area. I've taken some courses in the church because we have a spiritual education school, but I'm still in an area of flux.

HAPPENSTANCE? FATE? OR BOTH?

I believe in karma because you can't just continue doing negative things and expect positivity. Your choices will somehow come back around. Moreover, I believe in fate. While I believe God has a plan for you, I also believe you can do things to alter your plan.

#GOALS

My plan was, *I'm in college*. Now there is one caveat because I also was in love, very much in love. Even though I was living on campus, I was in D.C, and so was he. That was a problem. I'm sure that was a contributing factor to everything. But I mean, I don't know what I was looking ahead to. I was not focused on college.

POST COLLEGE

I ended up withdrawing from school, and I felt embarrassed. I felt a little bit like a failure. Had I been putting my nose to the grindstone and focused on my studies, I probably would have felt like I did my best. But in my heart of hearts, I knew I did not do my best. I felt I wasted an opportunity.

COLLEGE IS...

In college you separate from who your parents have groomed you to be a certain individual and begin to discover who you are. College is a safe place where you can make that transition. Because you are in college, you are still a child and your parents still care for you and support you from a distance. By attending college you can live an adult life without all the responsibility. Due to this, students need to go to college because it is a safe space where they can transition from child to adult.

MY PHILOSOPHY

Although college is a safe place, and I think it's really good for most people, it is not for everyone. So I think you need to evaluate whether you want to go. Take a hard look at the reasons on either side. Also, parents need to relax. After all, their child may not make it out of college in four years because, again, they are growing and learning who they are. Their college journey could take over four years. You don't want it to take ten, but it can certainly take five before their kid even gets a sense of what in the world is going on. Life lesson: Go to college. Enjoy that journey.

Tassie

UNIVERSITY OF MARYLAND, B.S. NUTRITIONAL
SCIENCE (CURRENTLY ATTENDING)

HOMETOWN: KINGSTON, JAMAICA

AGE GROUP: 30s

Life Motto: " *(1) Someday is not today. (2) The most powerful weapon on earth is the human soul and heart, so make sure that whatever you do in this life's journey, your soul is ignited with passion toward it.*"

LIFE BEFORE COLLEGE

When I was a teenager, I wanted to be a fashion designer. One time in the summer, I drew fashion designer sketches for a big fashion "house" back in Jamaica, and she loved my sketches. But I never had the passion for pursuing fashion. My passion is to open my own marketing company.

COLLEGE OR NAH?

I attended college for personal gain. I knew I would be the second person in my family to have earned a college degree. I wanted to go to college because I believe education is the key to success, although it doesn't have to be. Many people fell out of college and became successful, which we've seen with Bill Gates and all these other people who are big and didn't come from college.

I was excited to start college. I thought, *I'm at college, this is new, I'm going to finish and have a blast.* I was excited at the prospect of walking across the stage and getting my degree. Meanwhile, you learn that getting a job out of college and being set for life is not a reality.

THE GREY AREA

The grey area is an area of uncertainty and unknowing. Being on your journey but not knowing if you are going to get to your final destination. Because life throws many curveballs, you are sometimes on an unpredicted path and led through some things that keep you from your destination. At times, I am in the grey area and wonder if I will ever see the light at the end of the tunnel.

I believe the grey area can be temporary or permanent. Temporary in the sense that if you don't have a spirit of determinacy, and to fight for what you want, you will always be in the grey. The grey area will be temporary until you learn a sense of self. Then you will realize who you are and what you want and you'll do everything in your power to get to where you need to go. The grey area doesn't have to be permanent if you align yourself with the universe, make smart decisions, and go after what your heart desires.

HAPPENSTANCE OR FATE? OR BOTH?

I believe in fate. I think if it's meant to be, it'll be. If I meet a person at a certain time, in a certain way, on a particular day, or whatever, I believe that it is going to happen. Fate brought it that way; the universe led it that way. Nothing you do or say can change it. I also believe if you are supposed to die in a car crash, you will die in a car crash. Fate meant it that way. If you are supposed to meet the love of your life tomorrow at 9 o'clock and fall in love, it's going to happen.

#GOALS

The plan I had for college was to work hard during my first year. Do everything I can because I want to be on the dean's list. Then, I would work to earn scholarships for the second year because I wanted to transfer to a four-year school.

POST COLLEGE

Unfortunately, I didn't get a chance to finish school. I felt very disappointed, frustrated, and angry with myself because I had to put school on hold to focus on other things that were going on in my life. I felt a sense of uncertainty. Would I start back? I wanted to start back. I knew I would eventually start back, but I hated that I had to go through the process again.

Even though I didn't finish when I planned to, I'm still excited at the potential, not the possibility. I know I am going to finish; I am going to do it. I still have the urge to walk across the stage with my degree.

These days, I'm working in the non-profit industry as a development associate. The company I work for helps inner-city kids have access to better education.

COLLEGE IS...

I view college as a must for everyone, but you don't necessarily have to attend college to become successful. Many people did not go to college and still make mogul money. Many people have gone to college and are making zero, zilch, nada. College is a necessary evil, but an evil that you can get away with not completing if you know how to make entrepreneurial moves.

MY PHILOSOPHY

If you can push through any obstacle you face in your personal life, push through it, but don't drop out of college. Because the older you get, the harder it is to get yourself back into the groove of school. So if you can do it when you are young and knock it out, do it when you are young and knock it out. Don't waste time, don't be idle. That's what I would say to my younger self , like get your stuff together, and push through all your obstacles, but I would also say if you truly feel college is not for you, don't force it. Do something for yourself, and please don't get a degree that you can't use. Get a practical degree, something that will be profitable. The thing you are passionate about, go do that on the side but do not waste FASFA money on a degree in liberal science, ancient Greek history, etc.

Zana

CALIFORNIA LUTHERAN UNIVERSITY '21, B.A.
MARKETING COMMUNICATION
HOMETOWN: VAN NUYS, LA, CALIFORNIA
AGE GROUP: 20s

Life Motto: *"Accept everything that's happening and be present with people. Be a relatable person and be happy."*

LIFE BEFORE COLLEGE

During my childhood, I experienced different cultures and learned different perspectives. Sometimes when you grow up, you think everybody is like your parents because that's all you know. Then you realize, *Oh, life is different. Some people are a lot more privileged and some are less privileged.* Neither of my parents went to college so I had to learn about the process of applying to school and getting jobs on my own. My parents didn't have that knowledge and background for school, so they couldn't help guide as much in those regards.

As a little girl, my dream was to be a singer. I wanted to be a singer so bad! I didn't sing or do talent shows, nothing like that.

To be a singer was a random dream. I was way too shy. I didn't believe I could do anything I wanted. I thought, *Okay, you will go to high school, you are going to go to college.* I didn't necessarily have a direct career path, and it wasn't until my junior year of high school I realized I did not have a plan.

One of my teachers asked me what I wanted to do, and I said I didn't know. She continued, "So you are just going to be floating in the wind?" And I was like, "I guess so."..and that was a reality check for me.

COLLEGE OR NAH?

I went to college because I knew my mom wanted me to go. I thought if I didn't go, what else was I going to do? Everyone around me was pretty much applying for colleges. Every counselor at school was hounding us and going through all of our applications. I figured it's in my face, so why not? I didn't have another plan and I didn't want to work a meaningless job.

Beginning college I was super nervous. I was more honestly concerned with not knowing anybody; I wasn't thinking about my classes. I also did not want to go through my classes and college experience alone, so I was more concerned with making friends.

THE GREY AREA

The grey area is all about transition. I'm still trying to figure out exactly my primary focus and what job I'm going after. Although I'm in the grey area, I don't think the grey area is permanent for me. I think I'll find my path because I am actively trying to find my path. I will not sit here hoping and waiting for something to happen. I'm going to go after what I want. I have no problem taking risks.

HAPPENSTANCE? FATE? OR BOTH?

I believe in both. Of course, we all need something to believe in, to get you through, to push you, to motivate you. But also ...sometimes things happen and you have no control over the situation.

#GOALS

The only goal I had was to get into college and get out. I didn't have a four-year plan. I went into college blindly. I was undecided, clouded, and lost.

POST COLLEGE

After my first year, I decided college wasn't for me. I remember sitting on my bed, talking to my dad, and telling him I was thinking about going into the Navy. He said, "Okay, let's go sign up," and that's what happened. That same day I signed up, and later emailed my advisor and said I wasn't coming back to college. I felt good because I wasn't wasting my life. I also felt like I should go back to school, but I knew I wasn't ready for school at that time. But now I am. I'm currently enrolled in school, and I'm not working. I am focusing on my studies and making sure I can handle that before tackling a job.

COLLEGE IS...

A journey. There are so many routes you can take. There are so many people you meet in college, and it's nice because you will meet people who all are searching for something, as opposed to when you are in high school and get stuck at a dead-end job, and the people don't want to be there. In college, I noticed people have a passion because they want to do something and are open-minded. Students in college are open to exploring and understanding.

MY PHILOSOPHY

Listen to people who are older than you and take their advice. I wish I had taken the advice given to me and believed in myself more. If I hadn't been so scared to do things, I would have had a better experience in college. Be fearless in what you do.

Brandon

Attended Sinclair Community College
and studied Political Science

Hometown: Dayton, OH

Age Group: 20s

Life Motto: *"Everything and everyone matters. Take everything seriously."*

LIFE BEFORE COLLEGE

My mother has always been a business owner and my father was always really good with his hands. I think my mother's whole grasp of entrepreneurship has always pushed me into owning my business.

One thing I noticed about my mom growing up was that she owned her own business as she was always willing to be agile and do things in different ways. She would update her business or even change and go different routes. She was someone that was able to talk to anyone. People as a whole just liked her. She taught me how to be a likable person. She also taught me about how molding my own business is important. I give credit for where I am right now fully to my mom.

I can't say I had much of an actual vision for my life as a young man. I didn't know what I was going to do or even had a clue. The age of thirteen was very different for me. I learned how to read late. For instance, I didn't learn how to read until my junior year of high school, so I went through life thinking I was a very stupid person. I was always in school where as long as I'm doing just well enough, the teachers would pass me along and ignore what was truly going on.

My mom and dad were always very busy when it came to work, so they didn't realize I was struggling academically. I grew up for most of my life, or most of my younger years, thinking I was stupid. It wasn't until my senior year of high school I realized I'm a fairly intelligent guy and it wasn't until then I started setting goals for my life and truly seeing visions for myself.

COLLEGE OR NAH?

Everybody said you were supposed to go to college, so I went. Although everybody in my family said it was mandatory, nobody was willing to help me pay for it.

When I started college, I felt out of place. I didn't have a positive school experience for most of my life. Don't get me wrong; I find school very important. I want my kids to find a lot more joy than I did. But I cannot look back at school and say, "Oh, I want to do that again."

THE GREY AREA

Life is not as clear as people try to portray it. People say go to school, get a good job, give back to the community and be a successful person and do all this other stuff and start a family. I guess the grey area for me would be where life takes place. We are told to do these things as kids, and everything will be fine if our parents told us to do it this way, but then life happens. It's not clear; it's difficult. Some days you don't know what you are doing, but you keep going anyway.

HAPPENSTANCE? FATE? OR BOTH?

Probably all the above. I think some things in life just happen. But one thing a very impactful person in my life told me years ago is to take everything that happened in life very seriously and realize that everything is important.

#GOALS

When I first started college, I majored in political science. My goal at the time was to be a politician, but I started out shaky. I was a young scholar, but my mom hadn't finished my FASFA, which messed me over, so I wasn't able to get financial aid. When I finally started college, I was behind because I had to drop my first classes which put me behind my completion rate for my degree. Which kind of put me in a weird state, even to this day. So I had a plan, but my plan fell apart and fell completely; not all of it was my fault.

POST COLLEGE

During the time I discontinued school, I was down-talked by a lot of people. People said I was a dropout and thought I wasn't going to be anything in life, pretty much. I always wanted to be in politics, and I still do. I always wanted to be in the US Senate, and part of that would mainly involve me in most scenarios going to law school. Now, I'm not opposed to going back to school and then going to law school at some point when I can afford it. At the moment, I know I'm disciplined enough to go back to school and pursue law.

Currently, I plan to work on my business and growing businesses around me, saving up money and buying other businesses to accrue wealth. For instance, I own a business, *Janitorial Cleaning Solutions*, and I manage my mother's company, a paint party studio in downtown Dayton. We recently had our grand ribbon-cutting ceremony. I teach motorcycle classes for the State of Ohio and Harley Davidson as one of their riding coaches. I'm doing a lot; my life has been great.

COLLEGE IS...

A place where you can gather and gain a lot of organized information positively at a cost.

I view college as a very positive tool used in the right way. But I think it's not explained well. If it's not used properly, college becomes a tool that hurts many people who don't know how to benefit from it.

MY PHILOSOPHY

Everything you do matters. Everything adds up. Take everything seriously. Learn who you are as a person and always keep going. Enjoy every day you can because, on the days that you can't, you can't control that.

Marcus

HOMETOWN: WASHINGTON, DC

AGE GROUP: 60s

Life Motto: *"Don't sweat the small stuff."*

LIFE BEFORE COLLEGE

My mother and father influenced my upbringing; they were hard-working parents who went to work every day, including my father who worked two jobs to support his large family. As a kid I was taught to depend on no one. Depend on yourself by providing adequate income where you can take care of yourself, and if you get married and have a family, you need to support your family.

As a kid, my dream was to be a naval aviator, a jet pilot. The movie *Top Gun* kind of influenced my decision to look into becoming a pilot. Either for the Air Force or the Navy. But when I looked into it, you had to have 20/20 vision, which I did not have because I wore glasses. I had to be 20/20 vision unprotected so that completely knocked my dreams to become an aviator out of the box.

Since I couldn't do that, I went to work for the federal government. I was elected the president of my union, which allowed me to train employees filing EEO (Equal Employment Opportunity) complaints and their representatives..and that started my EEO career.

COLLEGE OR NAH?

Everybody suggested that when you get out of high school, go directly to college, and if you don't know what you want to major in, just take your basic courses to get started as your education from high school is still fresh in your mind.

Since nobody in my family went to college because they couldn't afford it, I didn't have a perspective of college. Once you get out of high school, in my family, you need to find a job. Luckily for me, I found a way to attend community college, which wasn't as expensive as a university.

THE GREY AREA

The grey area for me was working in EEO. Having a career in EEO was not anything that was in my plans. It was a happenstance that I was thrown into the EEO universe. I didn't know what I wanted to do professionally after being discouraged with my pilot dreams. The only thing I could think of was to make enough money I could with the skills that I had. So I would do various jobs that I could do that paid the most money. So if being a trash collector out in the street picking up the trash in front of your house paid more than being an EEO director, I would have done that also. It was always about the money, to take care of myself and my family. I was not career-oriented.

HAPPENSTANCE? FATE? OR BOTH?

I believe in both. Because I shouldn't be in this position. I am in this position because of what others saw in my capabilities. If you were working with me and watching how you work, I might say, "You know what? You would make a great attorney. Go to law school because you could make a great attorney." That wasn't your plan, but if you say, "Okay, everyone keeps saying I'll make a great attorney. Let me look at that." And then that direction pushes you into the destiny of being an attorney; even though that's not what you were looking to do, you became a great attorney.

POST COLLEGE

When I dropped out of school, I thought I would have to work a medical job. Because I'm not graduating with a degree in law, the medical field, philosophy, or psychology. So what professions are out there for a person without a college degree? Construction, which I did. These days, I am currently working for the federal government.

MY PHILOSOPHY

Some have the knack to make it through life without a college degree. If you do not go to college, there are other ways to educate yourself and live a good life.

Emmett

ATTENDED THE ART INSTITUTE OF ATLANTA AND
STUDIED MUSIC BUSINESS MANAGEMENT

HOMETOWN: DAYTON, OH

AGE GROUP: 70s

Life Motto: *"Do what you need to do."*

LIFE BEFORE COLLEGE

I always loved music, and my music teacher in grade school took a liking to my voice. I went to Miami chapel where they chose two kids from each grade level to appear down at Patterson Co-op. It was a year-round march of the year, and we would sing. Everybody who would perform were singers; I kind of had fun competing like that. I loved music and stayed with that on my way to high school, and that's where I ran into an old buddy of mine. His name is Emmett North, and he played lead guitar for Barry White and Isaac Hayes. I would go with him to places to listen to his band play. I used to have to use my cousin I.D. to get into some places we were playing because I was young.

TALK GREY TO ME

The band was the Night Rockets that Emmett North was playing with. He had a brother who looked and danced like James Brown. We called him Tweety; we got to be good friends. Then later, the band broke up, and Emmett North joined the Army. Tweety ended up singing for the Ohio Players when it first started, and he was the one who clued me in the group. We wound up being friends for life.

If I'd stayed with them, which was the plan, I was to go on tour and come back. I told my woman about it, and she said okay. Well, that's what she said *before* we got married. About a week or two after we got married, she told me not to go back to the band.

As for instilled principles, my parents told me to stay out of trouble, don't lie, and don't steal. A man should always look out for his kids. Then some of that other stuff about being a good husband and all that and being in church all the time. I believe in God, but I'm not in church all the time. But considering what I've seen by most, I'm a darn good father, I got that part down.

I was taught to think about priorities, and my parents told me I could be anything I wanted to be.

My dream as a young man was to perform music, be on stage, and also become an attorney. Once computers started coming on the scene, I got a real interest in that. Unfortunately, I couldn't get any of the elders or the grownups in my family to support me with it because they knew nothing about it; they thought it was just some kind of passing thing. I wanted to become a computer analyst, and when I took that to them, they didn't understand it, so I didn't pursue it.

COLLEGE OR NAH?

I graduated in January that year, and then I got hired at Wright Patt. Then, a few months later, I got married, so I didn't go to college straight out of high school.

I had lost my sister, and I wasn't handling it well. I was getting into fights almost every time I went out. I decided one day that I needed to get away from Ohio and away from everybody I knew until I got myself together.

I knew I needed something positive. So I thought about places I've been on tour, and one place I had the most fun was Atlanta. About 3-4 days after I came to that conclusion, an advertisement came on TV talking about The Art Institute of Atlanta. One major they had was music business management. I said, well, I'm already doing that, so I can just breeze through this one, plus keep my mind occupied. I applied and got in.

#GOALS

I planned to get through it and see if there was anything new to add to what I already knew. I also planned to connect with many people in entertainment down in Atlanta and possibly considered opening a booking agency there. It was not long until I was booking gigs out of my apartment.

THE GREY AREA

The grey area is kind of dormant. It's an area where I'm not going backwards, but I'm also not going forward—kind of like a state of suspended animation. Time is moving around you.

For the moment, I'd say I'm in a grey area. I'm not doing all of the stuff that I want to do because of my health. I should be out of the grey area once I get my health under control.

The grey area is either temporary or permanent, depending on the person. For me, it's temporary. Some people don't have any ambition, and it's like they spend their life rubbing the imaginary lamp with the genie in it. Ain't no genie coming out. They always make excuses for why they will not do what they want to do. These people transfer all blame on somebody else, as far as why they are not doing what they need to do. I'm not like that.

HAPPENSTANCE OR FATE? OR BOTH?

I believe in prep and do. First, you have to know where you want to go, look at where you are at, and prepare yourself to transition from where you are to where you want to go. The more you prepare yourself, the less of a problem you will have along your journey.

COLLEGE IS....

Advanced education for a person to further their tune and help them understand where they want to go as far as a career and see different things about what career they choose. College is also a great door opener for a lot of companies and government positions.

MY PHILOSOPHY

Have dedication and see things through. Be determined and have tenacity. Keep your health and stick to your diet. See a doctor at least once a year. Believe in God. Try to find a church you can go to. Keep educating yourself. Use discernment. Some people are emotional vampires; avoid those types of people.

End Word

Just as,

> *"The oak sleeps in the acorn,*
> *the giant sequoia tree sleeps in its tiny seed,*
> *the bird waits in the egg,*
> *God waits for his unfoldment in man."*

… the graduate stems from the student,
The adult springs from the child.

While transitioning from one stage to another, tune into you and enjoy the ride.

Play on, Children.

Ready to Talk Grey?
Grab your inner circle and have a seat.

Go to talkgreytome.com to purchase your own
Talk Grey To Me question cards.

Website: talkgreytome.com
IG: @talkgreytome (DM to request to be featured)

About the author:

M'Kai Folley lives in Washington, DC. Before writing this book, she earned an undergraduate degree in Mathematics from Xavier University. After that, she earned a graduate degree in Security Policy Studies from George Washington University just to shake things up. She was also a substitute teacher for a year and a half. She is now a working professional in Washington, DC and wrote this book in her in-between time during internships and substitute teaching.

If you are interested in learning more about M'Kai Folley and would like to be featured in Talk Grey To Me, please visit her website at http://talkgreytome.com or on Instagram, where you can sign up to receive an email when she is ready to conduct and schedule interviews.

IG: @talkgreytome

www.ingramcontent.com/pod-product-compliance
Lightning Source LLC
Chambersburg PA
CBHW071429070526
44578CB00001B/41